Level 5

Learning with Computers

Diana M. Trabel, M.Ed.
Trabel Educational Consulting
Sunman, IN

Jack P. Hoggatt, Ed.D.
Professor of Business Communications
University of Wisconsin
Eau Claire, WI

THOMSON
SOUTH-WESTERN

Australia · Canada · Mexico · Singapore · Spain · United Kingdom · United States

THOMSON
SOUTH-WESTERN

Learning with Computers, Level 5

Diana M. Trabel, Jack P. Hoggatt

VP/Editorial Director:
Jack W. Calhoun

VP/Editor-in-Chief:
Dave Shaut

Senior Publisher:
Karen Schmohe

Acquisitions Editor:
Jane Congdon

Development House:
Victory Productions, Inc.

Director Educational Marketing:
Carol Volz

Marketing Manager:
Michael Cloran

Marketing Coordinator:
Linda Kuper

Production Editor:
Martha Conway

Production Manager:
Tricia Boies

Manufacturing Coordinator:
Charlene Taylor

Media Developmental Editor:
Matthew McKinney

Media Production Editor:
Ed Stubenrauch

Design Project Manager:
Stacy Jenkins Shirley

Production House:
Victory Productions, Inc.

Cover Designer:
Brenda Grannan,
Grannan Graphic Design

Cover and Internal Illustrations:
Brenda Grannan

Internal Designer:
Brenda Grannan,
Grannan Graphic Design

Printer:
Quebecor World, Dubuque
Dubuque, Iowa

Printed in the United States of America
1 2 3 4 5 6 07 06 05 04 03

ISBN: 0-538-43542-9

For more information contact South-Western,
5191 Natorp Boulevard,
Mason, Ohio, 45040.
Or you can visit our Internet site at:
http://www.swlearning.com

About the Authors

Diana Trabel has been actively involved in elementary education and computer education for more than 25 years. After ten years as an elementary classroom teacher, Diana brought her classroom experience to curriculum development at South-Western/Thomson Learning. Currently, Diana is an author and educational consultant in the field of computer education. Diana is the co-author of the *Teacher's Resource Guide* for *Bernie's Typing Travels*, a program for teaching keyboarding to elementary students. *Learning with Computers* is the result of Diana's many years of working in education and publishing on how to make computers and software applications accessible and meaningful to all teachers and students.

Dr. Jack Hoggatt has taught Keyboarding at the elementary, middle, and high school levels. He also has taught Keyboarding methods courses and workshops for teachers. Dr. Hoggatt has been an author of South-Western Keyboarding products for the past 18 years, most recently contributing his expertise to *Bernie's Typing Travels*. Dr. Hoggatt is involved with his community and the school activities of his four children.

Dedication

I want to dedicate this book to my husband, Daniel. Without his encouragement and support I would never have reached my goal of becoming a teacher and I wouldn't be writing this book today. My deepest thanks go to some of my "homegrown" testers — my grandchildren — Jessica, Austin, Miranda, and Nichole. Thanks for working through my projects and giving me some great insight and ideas! Diana

Acknowledgements

Comments from reviewers of *Learning with Computers* have been valuable in the development of this book. Special thanks to the following individuals:

Jill Fioriello
Frank P. Long Intermediate School
Bellport, NY

Stacey Golightly
Ada High School
Ada, OK

Rebecca J. Kisner
Prairie Hills Middle School
Buhler District #313
Hutchinson, KS

Gladys B. McKinnon
W. G. Sanders Middle School
Columbia, SC

Donna Neward
Grace Lutheran School
Sandy, UT

Karen Roper
Center Middle School
Monaca, PA

Walter M. Sharpe, Ph.D.
Adjunct Assistant Professor
The Ohio State University
Columbus, OH

Kristi Trimboli
Baldwin Elementary
Rochester, MI

To the Student

Welcome to *Learning with Computers*, Level 5! In this book, you will find 18 interesting, engaging projects that will help you learn how to use the computer.

Several friendly characters will guide you through the steps of each project. Bernie, a mouse, will even travel with you in a Time Machine. You will visit Boston, Massachusetts, in 1773 and witness the Boston Tea Party. Also, you will travel back in time to 1910 to talk with Thomas Alva Edison. Your skills with graphics will help you create a timeline to show at a glance what he invented and when he invented it. Professor Keys, a scientist, will help Bernie explain the content of each project.

The book begins with an introduction to computer basics. You might already know the names of some of the parts of a computer, but you will learn more! Next, you will learn about word processing. This knowledge will help you create interesting reports, tables, and invitations. You will learn how to create and save documents; use different fonts, font styles, and font colors; cut, copy, and paste text; use the spelling checker; and even insert graphics into your documents.

After you have mastered word processing skills, you will learn how to use the Internet and e-mail. Next, you will learn how to create and run a slide show. After adding graphics, transitions, and music, your audience will really enjoy your show! Projects using spreadsheets and databases are also included in this book. Spreadsheets are a fun way to solve math problems, and databases will help you keep track of important information.

Each project begins with a list of computer skills and new vocabulary words, which are also included in the Glossary at the end of the book. Professor Keys or Bernie will provide step-by-step directions for completing each project. Helpful software screens will assist you along the way as you follow the directions.

In addition, each project also contains a one-page lesson to help you develop good keyboarding skills. Learning the touch-typing skills on the keyboarding pages will help you use a computer with ease.

Health and safety are critical parts of computer learning and use, so you will learn how ergonomics are important while using a computer. Bernie's friend Jake will introduce ergonomics tips in each project. Pay attention to these tips to build good habits. These tips will even help you when you play video games!

Jess, Bernie's little sister, drives a blue convertible named Blueberry. She loves that car! At the end of each project, Jess and Blueberry will take you on side trips for more activities in language arts, math, science, social studies, art, music, and health.

So join Bernie, Professor Keys, Jake, and Jess! They are ready to teach you all about computers!

Contents

Project 1 **Getting Started** Computer Basics and Word Processing **1**

Computer Skills • Identify the parts of a computer • Distinguish between hardware and software • Use correct posture at the keyboard • Open a file • Select, insert, and delete text • Save and print a file

Side Trips Art, Language Arts

Project 2 **A Great Report About a Great Invention** Word Processing **10**

Computer Skills • Locate folders and files • Insert page numbers • Delete folders and files

Side Trips Language Arts, Social Studies

Project 3 **The Recipe** Word Processing **17**

Computer Skills • Create, name, and save a file • Use proofreader's marks • Insert numbers and bullets • Use the thesaurus

Side Trips Language Arts, Health

Project 4 **The Great Debate** Word Processing **27**

Computer Skills • Create a table • Use the Copy and Paste commands • Format a table

Side Trips Art, Language Arts

Project 5 **Smile!** Word Processing **38**

Computer Skills • Use the thesaurus • Use the Find/Change or Replace command • Change the margins • Set tabs • Change fonts

Side Trips Language Arts

Project 6
All About E-mail Internet **49**

Computer Skills • Use e-mail • Identify the parts of an e-mail message • Send e-mail • Receive e-mail • Reply to e-mail

Side Trips Social Studies, Language Arts

Project 7
Searching the Internet Internet and Word Processing .. **60**

Computer Skills • Use the Internet • Enter a URL • Use toolbar buttons to navigate the Internet • Set an Internet bookmark • Use a search engine

Side Trips Language Arts, Social Studies

Project 8
Read All About It! Word Processing **72**

Computer Skills • Insert a date • Set page orientation • Set margins • Create columns • Insert a graphic

Side Trips Language Arts, Math

Project 9
Colonial Workers Internet and Word Processing **81**

Computer Skills • Use electronic reference tools • Multitask between two open programs • Cite a source • Format a document • Set text in three columns • Use the spelling checker

Side Trips Social Studies

Project 10
The Timeline Graphics and Multimedia **91**

Computer Skills • Use design and layout skills • Use draw tools • Add text to a timeline

Side Trips Social Studies, Art

Project 11
Science in the Garden Graphics and Multimedia **99**

Computer Skills • Create a slide show • Change backgrounds • Insert graphics • Use transitions between slides • Set the time to advance slides • Move a slide

Side Trips Science, Language Arts

Project 12
Uncle Sam Graphics and Multimedia **111**

Computer Skills • Create a slide show • Use a template • Cite sources • Add transitions and timing • Insert audio and graphics

Side Trips Social Studies, Language Arts

Project 13 **Figure It Out** Spreadsheet **121**

Computer Skills • Enter data in a spreadsheet • Use a spreadsheet to solve problems • Use the Average formula • Format a spreadsheet • Add charts

Side Trips Math

Project 14 **What's for Lunch?** Spreadsheet **135**

Computer Skills • Create a spreadsheet • Use a spreadsheet to solve problems • Delete a column • Insert a line graph • Add shading • Center text • Format text

Side Trips Health, Music

Project 15 **Road Trip!** Spreadsheet **149**

Computer Skills • Use a spreadsheet to solve problems • Insert data in a spreadsheet • Use formulas • Add borders and shading

Side Trips Language Arts, Math

Project 16 **Across America** Database **162**

Computer Skills • Use a database • Add data • Insert, modify, and delete a field • Search for data

Side Trips Social Studies, Health

Project 17 **Student Profiles** Database **174**

Computer Skills • Insert a field • Add data • Insert a record • Delete a field • Delete a record • Move a field • Sort data

Side Trips Science, Language Arts

Project 18 **A Bright Idea** Database **184**

Computer Skills • Create a database • Insert fields and records • Sort data • Use electronic reference tools • Add data • Multitask using two programs

Side Trips Science, Art

Glossary **G1**

Project 1

Computer Basics and Word Processing

Getting Started

In this project you will:

- Identify the parts of a computer
- Distinguish between hardware and software
- Use correct posture at the keyboard
- Open a file
- Select, insert, and delete text
- Save and print a file

Word Power

CD-ROM drive
CPU
disk drive
ergonomics
hardware
keyboard
monitor
mouse
program
software

Side Trips with Blueberry and Jess

Science

Create Create a database to focus on modern inventions in the last twenty-five years. Cell phones and palm pilots are new inventions. Personal computers would at the top of the list. Use the fields *Invention, Date Invented,* and *Purpose of Invention*. Include at least four records in your database. Use the Internet, a reference CD-ROM, or an online encyclopedia to research the information. Save your database as *new inventions18*.

Art

Create Create a database about five famous artists and their works. Set up your fields before you begin your research. Use the fields *Last Name, First Name, Place of Birth, Dates,* and *Famous Works*. You can also add a field called *Comments*. Express your feelings about the artworks in this field. Use the Internet, a reference CD-ROM, or an online encyclopedia to research the information. Save your database as *artists18*.

Revise a Form

Welcome to my computer lab! I have been waiting for you. Are you ready to learn about computers? Come inside! Sit down at a computer. I will explain the different parts of a computer and introduce you to some programs you will use. I will give you a list of rules to follow when you are in the lab. We have a lot to do, so let's get started!

PART 1

All About Hardware and Software

Look at the computer in front of you. What do you see? What can you touch? Things that you can touch are called hardware.

- The monitor is at eye level. This is where the computer displays, or shows, your work.
- The mouse is attached to the keyboard.
- The CPU, which stands for **central processing unit**, is the "brains" of the computer. It makes the computer run and carries out the instructions you give it.

You are learning fast! Now, can you locate the disk drive and the CD-ROM drive? These drives are hardware, too.

Bernie's Typing Activities

Key each drill line twice; key each paragraph once.

Skill Building

numbers

1 Rooms 173 and 306 were cleaned on May 2.

2 Rooms 148 and 359 were cleaned on May 3.

balanced-hand sentences

3 Jan Cox and I may burn the wood or coal.

4 Vivian may suspend all eight of the men.

5 He owns the antique bottle on the shelf.

Which Park Am I?

I am a national park located in the Black Hills of South Dakota. I average 2.6 million visitors a year.

Visitors can see the faces of four Presidents chiseled in rock. Each of the faces is about 60 feet tall. Which park am I?

Here is a riddle: Why is a computer like a TV? Answer: **Because both are useless without programs.** ***Computer programs are called the software. They operate with the hardware to make the computer run. With the right software, you can use the computer to write, draw, do math, and communicate with people just about everywhere on Earth!***

In this book, you will use software programs to create all kinds of documents like book reports, outlines, spreadsheets, databases, and slide shows. You will also tap into your creativity and add graphics and audio to your projects!

Quick Check

Which of the following are hardware? Which are software?

spreadsheet	disk drive	keyboard
mouse	slide show	CPU
monitor	printer	cable

Excellent! I am so glad you are in my class!

1. Open your reference CD-ROM or a search engine in your Internet browser program.
2. In the Search box, type *Alexander Bell*.
3. Click on an article and skim it to find the facts you need to complete the database.
4. Navigate to your database program and enter the data.
5. Save your work.

Use the **Restore Down** or **Zoom** button to see both programs at once.

To view the full screen again, click on the button again.

Restore Down button

Continue your research. Return to your reference source and search for the other inventors on your database.

Quick Check

Excellent work! Your database should look like this.

Last Name	First Name	Date of Birth	Date of Death	Inventions
Bell	Alexander	1847	1922	telephone
Eastman	George	1854	1932	rolled film
Edison	Thomas	1847	1931	phonograph
Fleming	Alexander	1881	1955	penicillin
Morgan	Garrett	1877	1963	gas mask

On Your Own

Add a new field called Place of Birth to your database. Then search for this information. You can follow the same steps you took to find your other data, or you might want to use a different source. Which source worked best for you?

PART 2

Ergonomics and You

Bernie is my best student and helper in the lab. Here is a picture of Bernie at the computer. You can see that he is putting the rules of good computer posture into practice.

- His shoulders are back, not rounded.
- His elbows are to the side, not raised.
- His wrists are low, but not resting on the keyboard.
- His feet are flat on the floor.

Good posture is important because not sitting correctly can result in injuries to your body. That is what ergonomics is about—the way people work with machines so that they do not harm themselves.

1. Click on the field name ***Last Name***.
2. Choose **Records**.
3. Click on the **Sort Ascending** or **Sort +** button on the toolbar.
4. Save the file.

Access AppleWorks

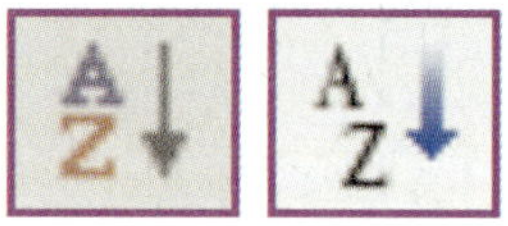

Quick Check

Terrific! The inventors' last names should now appear in alphabetical order. If they do not, make the changes now.

Last Name	First Name	Date of Birth	Date of Death	Inventions
Bell	Alexander			
Eastman	George			
Edison	Thomas			
Fleming	Alexander			
Morgan	Garrett			

PART 4

Facts at Our Fingertips

Now we can get started on our research. Some computers have an encyclopedia that comes on a CD-ROM. You can open the encyclopedia and search for information. You can also go the Internet. I used the search engine at www.google.com. A dictionary is also a useful reference work for finding dates of people's lives.

But what if you have problems holding the correct posture? It could be you need a little something extra to help you. So . . .

- If your feet don't touch the floor . . .
  . . . rest your feet on some books or blocks.
- If your shoulders are rounded . . .
  . . . you may need a pillow to support your back.
- If your eyes are not level with the text on the monitor . . .
  . . . you may need a cushion to sit on.

PART 3

Sign on the Dotted Line

All the students in my lab must follow a few simple rules when they use a computer. You can sign a form letter that I give to all my students. I call it a Responsible Use Form. When you sign this form letter, you are promising me that you will use computers responsibly.

1. Open your word processor.
2. Select the **File** menu and choose **Open**.
3. Choose the file named *letter*, and click on the **Open** button.

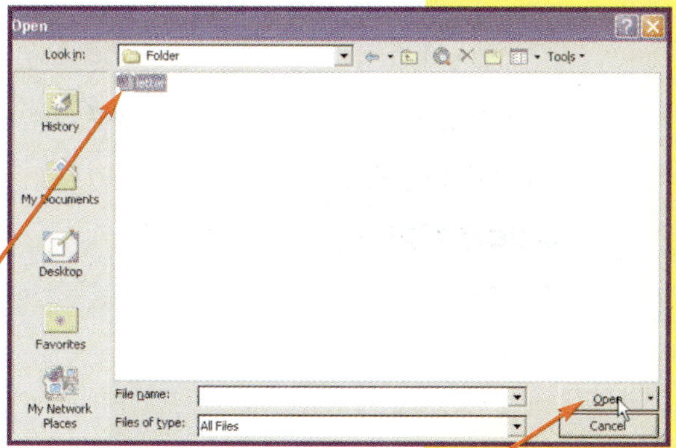

Choose the file named *letter.*

Click on the **Open** button.

Now use my notes to add the first and last name of the other inventors. Be sure to start with the last name!

Alexander Bell
Thomas Edison
Garrett Morgan
George Eastman
Alexander Fleming

Be sure to capitalize the first letter of each proper noun.

6 Save the file.

Quick Check

Your Access database should look something like this. If it does not, make the changes now.

	inventors18ID	Last Name	First Name	Date of Birth	Date of Death	Inventions
	1	Bell	Alexander			
	2	Edison	Thomas			
	3	Morgan	Garrett			
	4	Eastman	George			
	5	Fleming	Alexander			

PART 3

Bring Some Order

Now that the database is set up, you can begin doing research to fill in the fields. To make the research process easier, let's sort the data in the **Last Name** *field so that the names are in alphabetical order.*

4. Select the **File** menu and choose **Save As**.
5. Type *letter1* in the **File name** box to name the file.
6. Click on the **Save** button.

Good job! Now take a few minutes to read the letter. As you can see, the letter is a form letter. We will make it personal by adding your teacher's name and your name to the letter. Follow my simple instructions!

7. Select the words ***your teacher's name***.
8. Select the **Edit** menu and choose **Cut**.
9. Type in your teacher's name.

10. Select the words ***the undersigned***.
11. Tap the **Delete** key.
12. Type in your name.

13. In the last bulleted statement, place the cursor before the word ***copyright***. Insert the word ***the***.

14. Select the words ***your name*** at the bottom of the letter.
15. Type in your name.
16. Save your work. Select the **File** menu and choose **Save**.

Congratulations! You are off to a good start.

When you start typing, the selected text will be replaced by the text you type.

PART 2

Names to Know

Thanks for helping me create the fields! Now let's add records to the table. We need to create five records.

Access

1. Move to the first record under the field named ***Last Name***. Type ***Bell***.
2. Strike the **Tab** key and move to the second field. Type ***Alexander***.
3. Move to the second record under the field named ***Last Name***. Type ***Edison***.
4. Strike the **Tab** key and move to the second field. Type ***Thomas***.

AppleWorks

1. Click in the record below the field named ***Last Name***. Type ***Bell***.
2. Strike the **Tab** key and move to the second field. Type ***Alexander***.
3. Choose **New Record** from the **Edit** menu.
4. Type ***Edison*** in the record that is automatically selected.
5. Strike the **Tab** key and move to the second field. Type ***Thomas***.

Good work!

*If you are using AppleWorks, you can also click on the **New Record** button on the toolbar. It looks like this.*

PART 4

Job Well Done!

You have been an excellent student! You have read my form letter and revised it by adding your teacher's name and your name. Now you need to sign the letter. Of course, you can't do that on the computer. We still need a pen and a piece of paper for that. So let's print the letter. Then we will save it to a folder.

1. Select the **File** menu and choose **Print**.
2. Click on **Print**.
3. Close the file.

Ask your teacher how to save the file to a folder on your computer. Listen carefully to the instructions. Your computer lab may be set up differently from mine.

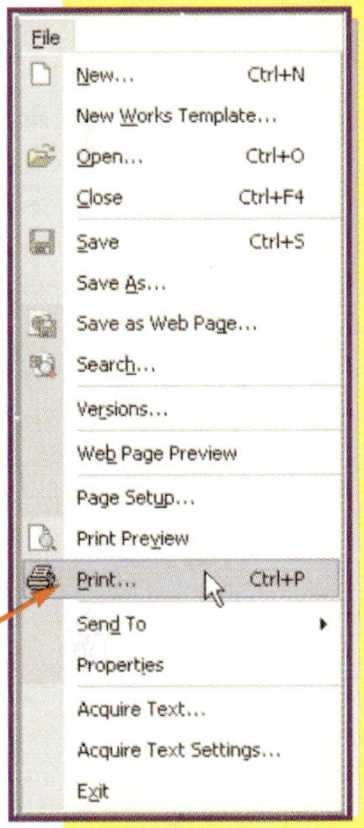

Choose **Print** from the **File** menu.

On Your Own

Compare the rules in your own school with Professor Keys' rules. Does your school have other rules? What are they? Add two additional rules that you follow in your own classroom when you use the computer.

Use my notes to add four more fields. These fields will give the categories of information that we will research. Here are the fields that we will use to guide our research.

Last Name
First Name
Date of Birth
Date of Death
Inventions

5. After you have added these fields, click on **Done**.
6. Choose **List** from the **Layout** menu.
7. Choose **Save** from the **File** menu.
8. Type *inventors18* in the **File name** box.
9. Click on **Save**.

Your database should look like this.

inventors18.cwk (DB)

Last Name	First Name	Date of Birth	Date of Death	Inventions

Jake's Ergonomics Tip

You may find that using an ergonomic keyboard reduces the strain on your hands and wrists while you work. Ergonomic keyboards usually have a split design with left and right banks and the ability to tilt the keyboard for comfort.

Bernie's Typing Activities

Open your word processor.
Key the drill lines.

Reinforce: a, s, d, f, j, k, l, ;, e, n, o, t

home row

1 dd aa ss ff jj ;; kk ll kd kd ;a ;a lflf
2 dd aa ss ff jj ;; kk ll kd kd ;a ;a lflf

3 sad all lad ads dad; ask; jak; fall; add
4 sad all lad ads dad; ask; jak; fall; add

e emphasis

5 fee see; feed leak seek; lake lead jade;
6 fee see; feed leak seek; lake lead jade;

n emphasis

7 an and knee den need lane sand fans land
8 an and knee den need lane sand fans land

o emphasis

9 no do so of son sod does loans done load
10 no do so of son sod does loans done load

t emphasis

11 to ten jet told tone took date foot task
12 to ten jet told tone took date foot task

all letters learned

13 lot sat food look jade neat often needle
14 lot sat food look jade neat often needle

16. Click on **Finish** to complete the table.
17. Save the file.

Quick Check

Your database should look like this. If not, make the changes now.

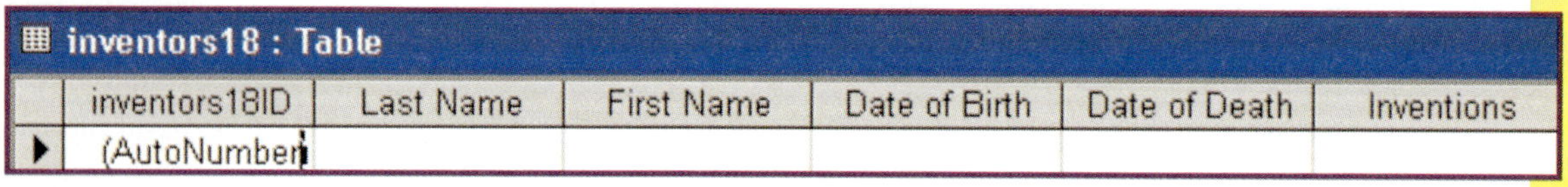

If you are using AppleWorks, follow these steps.

1. Open AppleWorks.
2. Choose **Database**.

We need to name the fields that will appear in our table. Our database will contain five fields. The first field will say* Last Name. *Let's create the first field now.

3. In the **Field Name** box, type ***Last Name***.
4. Click on **Create**.

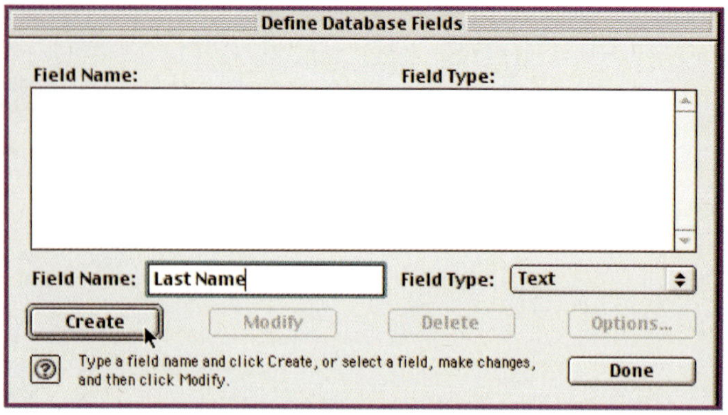

***Good work! You now have one field named* Last Name.**

Side Trips with Blueberry and Jess

Art

Illustrate Ask family members and friends to describe safety rules they follow as they work, whether on the job or in their home. Create a poster on the computer that explains why such rules are important.

Language Arts

Write Write a letter to Professor Keys and Bernie. Introduce yourself, and tell what you already know about computers. Tell them how you have used the computer. Then explain what you would like to learn about computers. For example, what would you like to learn how to do or to do better? Use the computer to type your letter. Save it as *myletter1*.

Use my notes to add four more fields. These fields give the categories of information that we will research.

Last Name
First Name
Date of Birth
Date of Death
Inventions

Quick Check

Does your list of fields look like this? If not, make the changes now.

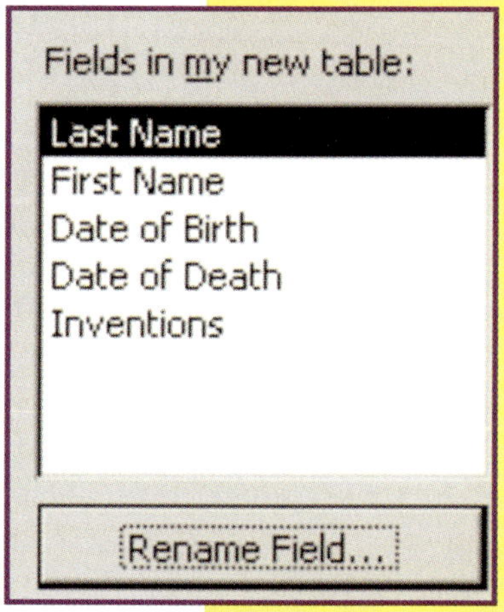

13. After you have completed your list of fields, click **Next**.
14. Name your table *inventors18*. Then click **Next**.
15. Select **Enter data directly into the table.**

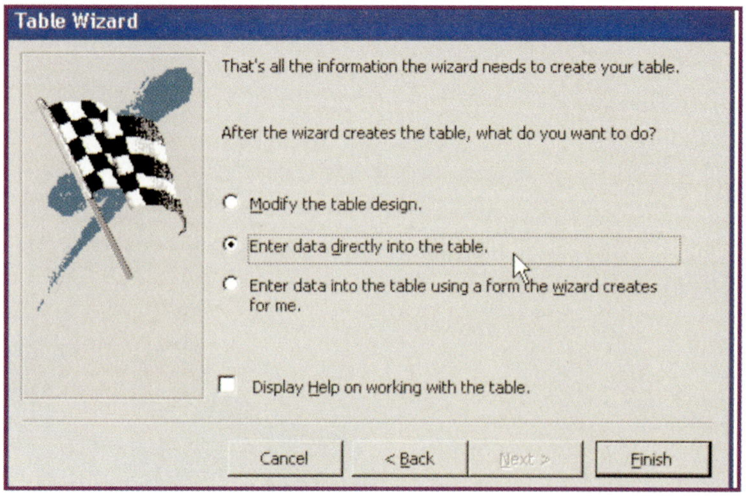

Project 2

Word Processing

A Great Report About a Great Invention

In this project you will:

- Locate folders and files
- Insert page numbers
- Delete folders and files

Word Power

file

folder

6 Choose **Personal** for the table category.

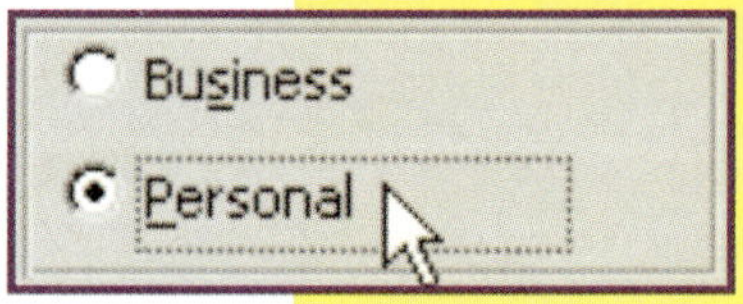

Wizard contains several kinds of tables that you might use to create a database. We are going to use the Categories table.

7 Click on **Categories** in the **Sample Tables** box.

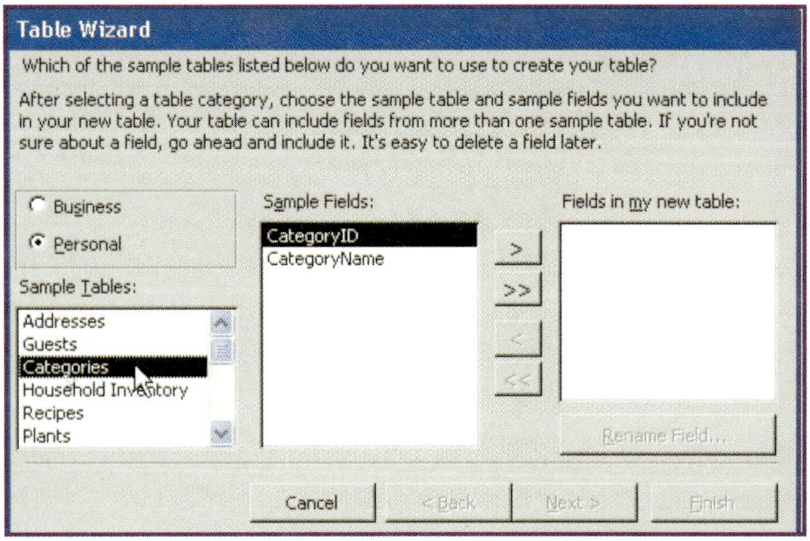

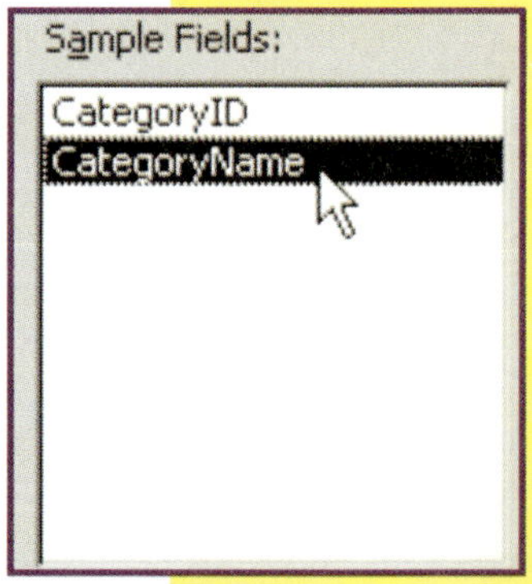

Now that we have set up the table, we need to add the fields. Our database will contain five fields. The first field will be* Last Name. *Let's create the first field now.

8 Click on **Category Name**.

9 Click on the **Right** arrow button to add a field.

10 Click on **Rename Field** to name the field.

11 In the **Field name** box, type *Last Name*.

12 Click on **OK**.

Click on **Rename Field**.

***Good work! You now have one field named* Last Name.**

Project 2

Locate a Folder and Files

I have written a report about the history of computers. I looked up information in books and on the Internet. I took notes on what I read, and then I made an outline based on my notes. I used my outline to write my first draft. Now, my final report just needs new margins and page numbers.

To keep my documents organized, I put them in folders, just like you probably do with your schoolwork. Of course, I did all of my work on the computer! Follow me, and I will show you how to create and locate folders and files. Let's go!

PART 1

Where Is It?

***I put my research report about computers in a folder called* Great Report. *I named the file* my report.**

Let's locate the folder and open it to find my report.

1. Go the **taskbar** and choose **Start**.
2. Choose **Search**, then choose **All files and folders**.

*If you are using a Mac, select the **File** menu and choose **Find**.*

3. In the **File** name box, type *inventors18*.
4. Click on **Create**.

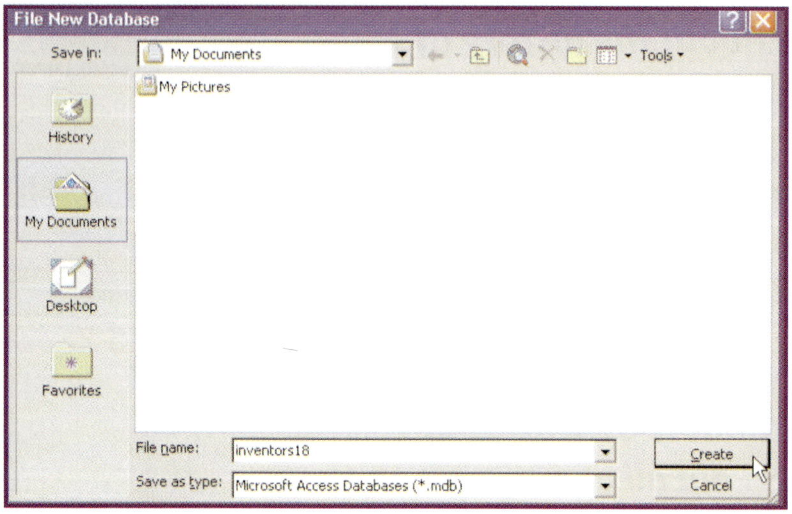

Now let's create a table for the database by using wizard. Wizard lets us choose from some common types of tables. Wizard has already done some of the work for us.

5. Select **Tables** from the **Database** window and double-click on **Create table by using wizard**.

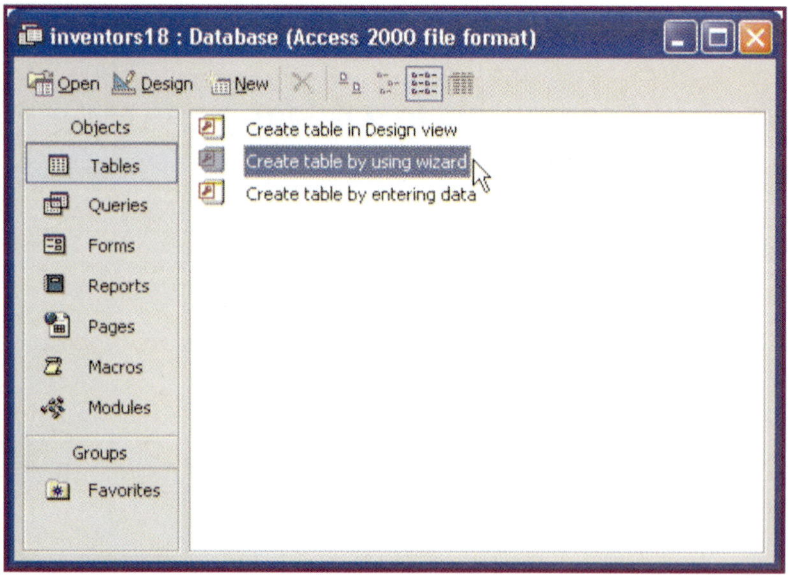

3. Enter the name of the folder that holds all my work by typing in *Great Report*. Then click on the **Search** button.
4. The search results appear on the right side of the window. The window shows the name and location of the folder.
5. Open the folder to see the documents inside it.

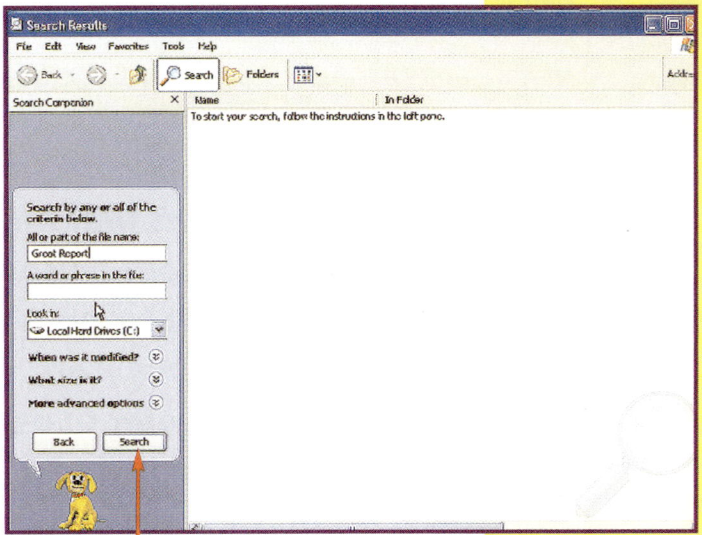

Click on the **Search** button.

You can see that I have another folder called* Research *within the* Great Report *folder. I put my background work—my notes and outline—in that second folder.

*You can use the **Find** feature to locate either a folder or a file.*

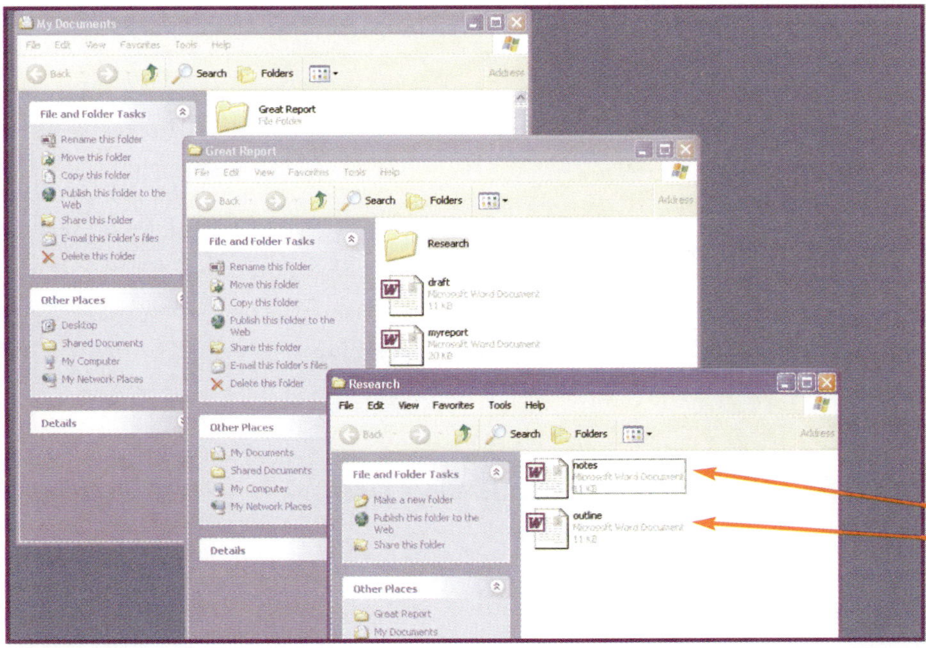

These files are in the folder named **Research**.

6. Double-click on *my report* to open the file.
7. Save the file as *my report2*.

Project 18

Create a Database About Famous Inventors

Think of all the inventions that have changed our lives. We learned about Edison's inventions in Project 10. Now I want to learn more about the lives of some other inventors. To keep track of all my information, I want to use a database. Each time I find a fact, I will add it to my database. A database is great way to organize information and keep facts at my fingertips! Will you help me? Together we will learn how to create a database and learn about some great inventors too. Let's get started!

PART 1

Creating a Database

The first step is to create the fields and records for the database.

If you are using Access, follow these steps. If you are using AppleWorks, go to page 189.

1. Open Microsoft Access.
2. Choose **Blank Database**.

PART 2

Page Number, Please

The computer makes it so easy to add page numbers! We will add our page numbers to the top left of our document.

Word

1. Select the **Insert** menu and choose **Page Numbers**.
2. Click on the drop-down arrow and select **Bottom of page**.
3. Click on the drop-down arrow and select **Center** from the **Alignment** box.
4. Click on **OK**.

AppleWorks

1. Choose **Insert Footer** from the **Format** menu.
2. Select the **Edit** menu and choose **Insert Page #. . .**
3. Click on **Page Number** if it is not already selected.
4. Click on **OK**.

I told you it was easy! Let's finish up.

1. Save your work.
2. Close the file.
3. Close your word processor.

Jake's Ergonomics Tip

Don't let your hand get cramped when you use the computer. Make a tight fist and hold it for a second. Then spread your fingers apart as far as you can. Hold them there for five seconds. Relax your hand. Repeat the exercise five times. And don't skip the relaxing part.

Project 18

Database

A Bright Idea

In this project you will:

- Create a database
- Insert fields and records
- Sort data
- Use electronic reference tools
- Add data
- Multitask using two programs

Word Power

database

field

record

sort

table

wizard

PART 3

Easy Come, Easy Go

Thanks for your help! My report is complete and I am sure Professor Keys will like it. Now that I have completed my report, I can delete my folder that contains my notes and outline.

1. Find the folder ***Research***.
2. Click on the folder ***Research*** and drag it to the **Recycle Bin**.
3. Click **Yes** to confirm that you want to delete it.

There is one more thing to delete: the file named **draft.** ***Drag it just the way you dragged the*** **Research** ***folder.***

If you would like to print out my report and learn more about the history of computers, check with your teacher.

On the Mac, you drag the folder to the ***Trash****.*

Never delete other people's folders or files without their permission.

On Your Own

Use the Search or Find command to search for the folder you just deleted. Does the computer say that it is in the Recycle Bin or Trash? If so, you did it correctly. Good work!

Side Trips with Blueberry and Jess

Science

Research Modify the *students17* database to create one about butterflies. Rename the records to include five records for types of butterflies. Then rename the fields *Origin, Life Span*, and *Color*. Delete the other two fields. Conduct your research by using the Internet or an electronic reference tool. Save your file as *butterflies17*.

Language Arts

Modify Choose one of your favorite books. Modify the *students17* database to create a database about the main characters in your book. Rename the fields with fields that describe your characters. Your fields should tell the name, age, description, and character traits of each character. Save your database as *characters17*.

If you are using Access, you will need to ask your teacher to make a copy of the students17 *database before you begin.*

Bernie's Typing Activities

Open your word processor.
Key the drill lines.

Reinforce: i, r, h, left shift, c, y

all letters learned

1 took; jade; last; food; safe; tent; lake
2 took; jade; last; food; safe; tent; lake

i emphasis

3 is it in if life knife join did toil lid
4 is it in if life knife join did toil lid

r emphasis

5 red are jar ran rake real fear dear rest
6 red are jar ran rake real fear dear rest

h emphasis

7 he the horn half heat hen hire hint heir
8 he the horn half heat hen hire hint heir

left shift emphasis

9 Jan Kent Lonnie Ollie Ida Ned Hank Janet
10 Jan Kent Lonnie Ollie Ida Ned Hank Janet

c emphasis

11 car can ace Jack race cried clear access
12 car can ace Jack race cried clear access

y emphasis

13 yes yarn yard year Kay Jay fry dryer say
14 yes yarn yard year Kay Jay fry dryer say

Bernie's Typing Activities

Key each drill line twice; key each paragraph once.

Skill Building

shift keys

1. Mr. and Mrs. Jones, Dr. Raquel Martinez;
2. Dr. Voss will be in San Diego on Monday.

balanced-hand sentences

3. They may wish to go with us to the city.
4. You may fix the big signs by the chapel.
5. The neighbor will pay for the oak chair.

Which Park Am I?

I am the first national park in the world. I was established on March 1, 1872. I am located in three different states.

I am the home of Old Faithful Geyser. I am the home to such wildlife as grizzly bears, bison, and elk. Which national park am I?

Side Trips with Blueberry and Jess

Language Arts

Write There are many names in Bernie's report on the history of computers. Choose one person and find out more about his life. Use the Internet or books from your library to do your research. Type your notes in your word processor. Create an outline. Then use the computer to write a brief biography. Explain the contribution he made to the development of computers.

Social Studies

Research What other important inventions besides the computer have changed the world? Consider, for example, the impact of the printing press. Where would we be without the telephone or electricity? Research other inventions, and create a timeline. Use your computer to type your timeline.

Great job! You have moved the field. Now let's sort the records in alphabetical order. Find the Sort Ascending button or Sort + button on the toolbar.

Access **AppleWorks**

3. Click on the field *Last Name*.
4. Click on the **Sort** button.
5. Save your work.

You did an excellent job with my database! You followed many steps to give me the database that I wanted.

*The **Sort Descending** or **Sort –** button puts the names in order from Z to A. Try it!*

Quick Check

Your database should look like this.

Last Name	First Name	M/F	Hobby	Career Goal
Jenkins	Pat	M	karate	writer
Ling	Mary	F	skating	figure skater
Mendez	Flora	F	painting	teacher
Nolan	Jon	M	baseball	hockey player

On Your Own

Join Professor Keys' class! Add a new record to students17. Include facts about yourself in the database. Then enter information about your own interests and career goals.

Project
3

Word Processing

The Recipe

In this project you will:

- Create, name, and save a file
- Use proofreader's marks
- Insert numbers and bullets
- Use the thesaurus

Word Power

bullet

thesaurus

I am sorry to say that Rina Chang is leaving the school. I need to delete her record from the database.

1. Click on Rina Chang's name in the database.
2. Choose **Delete Record** from the **Edit** menu.
3. Save your work.

Quick Check

Fantastic! Your database should look like this.

First Name	Last Name	M/F	Hobby	Career Goal
Pat	Jenkins	M	karate	writer
Flora	Mendez	F	painting	teacher
Jon	Nolan	M	baseball	hockey player
Mary	Ling	F	skating	figure skater

PART 4

From A to Z

Thanks for helping with my database. I need to make two changes. I want to move the field* Last Name *before the field* First Name*. Then I want to sort, or put the names in alphabetical order.

Let's start with the first step and move the field* Last Name*. If you are using AppleWorks, you must be in List layout. Choose List from the Layout menu.

In Access, click on the field name to select the column. Click again and drag the field when you see a small outline of a rectangle. Then you know you have got it!

1. Click on the field *Last Name*.
2. Drag the field to the *First Name* field.

Project
3

Type a Recipe

I love to collect recipes. Every time I eat something good at a friend's house, I ask for the recipe. But now I have too many recipes that I scribbled down on scraps of paper. I have decided to put all my recipes on the computer. That way, I can always find a recipe when I want to make it.

My friend's recipe for Creepy Caterpillar is on the next page. I have proofread it. Will you type the recipe on the computer, making the changes I have made? You might even want to make this recipe yourself!

PART 1

Food for Thought

We need to create a new file and name it. Then we can type the recipe in this new file. Let's get started!

1. Turn on your computer and click on the word processor icon. This opens a new file.
2. Type the name of your recipe—*Creepy Caterpillar*.
3. Save the file as *recipe3*.

It looks like I have a great addition to my class and you have made a great addition to the database!

Quick Check

Does your database look like this? If not, recheck your work.

First Name	Last Name	M/F	Grade	Hobby	Career Goal
Rina	Chang	F	5	swimming	firefighter
Pat	Jenkins	M	5	karate	writer
Flora	Mendez	F	5	painting	teacher
Jon	Nolan	M	5	baseball	hockey player
Mary	Ling	F	5	skating	figure skater

PART 3

Changes, Changes

All my students this year are in the fifth grade, so I want to delete the field for grade. Can you do this for me?

Access

1. Select the field *Grade*.
2. Choose **Delete Column** from the **Edit** menu.
3. Click on **Yes** to delete the field.

AppleWorks

1. Choose **Define Fields** from the **Layout** menu.
2. Select the field *Grade*.
3. Click on the **Delete** button.
4. Click on **OK**.
5. Click on **Done**.

4 Now, type the recipe.

Be sure to make my changes that I marked on the copy. The proofreader's marks are shown in the box to help you identify them.

CREEPY CATERPILLAR

Equipment

plate

butter knife

Ingredients

peanut butter (or other nut butter)

banana

raisins

chow mein noodles

lettuce

Directions

Tear off one lettuce leaf and set on ~~a~~ the plate.

Lay peeled banana on the leaf⊙

slice the banana into 1/2-inch chunks.

Use nut butter to stick the slices back together.

Use ~~razins~~ raisins for the eyes.

Use noodles for mouth, and feelers.

Serving Suggestions

Serve as a ~~snak~~ snack, light lunch, or dessert⊙

One caterpillar is a single serving.

It's delicious!

^	Insert
→	Move
~~out~~	Delete
¶	Start a new paragraph
d (triple underline)	Capitalize
my ~~C~~at	Lowercase
⊙	Insert a period

5 Use the spelling checker to check your work.

6 Save the file.

PART 2

Meet a New Student

I have just received a letter from a new student. She is going to join my class. We need to create a new record for her. Her letter contains all the information I need for my database. Can you fill in her record for me?

> Dear Professor Keys,
>
> Thank you for welcoming me to your school. I am in the fifth grade. My favorite hobby is skating because I hope to be a figure skater when I grow up.
>
> Sincerely,
>
> Mary Ling

Access

1. Choose **New Record** from the **Insert** menu.

AppleWorks

1. Choose **New Record** from the **Edit** menu.

2. Move to the empty row under ***First Name.*** Type ***Mary***.
3. Use the **Tab** key to move to the next field and type ***Ling***.
4. Continue typing the data from Mary's letter for the next fields.
5. Save your work.

*In AppleWorks, you can click on the **New Record** button on the toolbar to add a new record.*

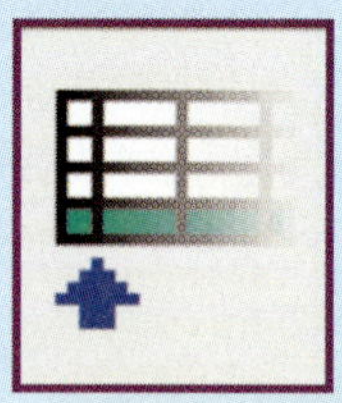

PART 2

It's as Easy as 1, 2, 3

We can make this recipe even easier to read by numbering the steps under Directions. We could just type in a number before each line. A quicker way, however, is to use the numbering function.

Word

1. Select the list of steps under ***Directions***.
2. Select the **Format** menu and choose **Bullets and Numbering**.
3. Click on the **Numbered** tab.
4. Click on the number style that looks like this: 1.
5. Click on **OK**.
6. Save your work.

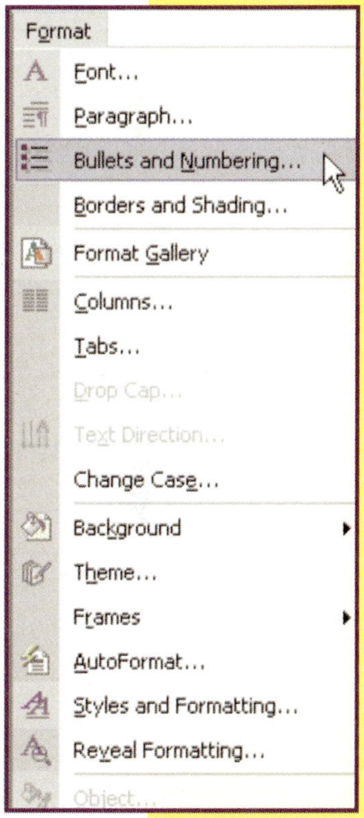

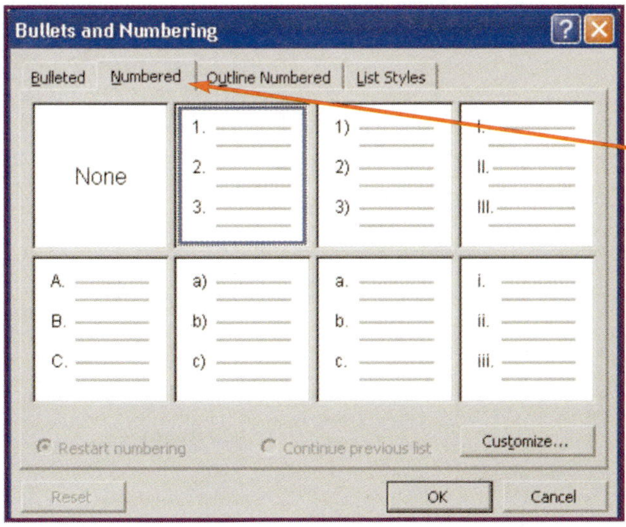

Click on the **Numbered** tab.

I asked my students to name their career goals, and here is what they told me. Let's add this information now to the new field you just created.

Rina Chang	firefighter
Pat Jenkins	writer
Flora Mendez	teacher
Jon Nolan	hockey player

*Use the **Tab** key or the arrow keys to move from record to record. In **Browse** layout in AppleWorks, you can click on the **Record** book to move from record to record.*

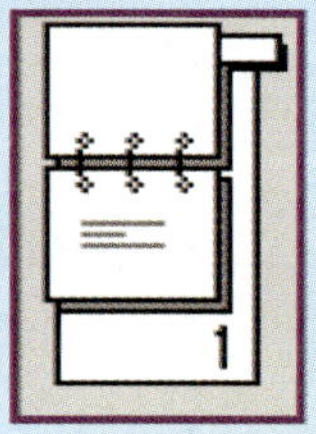

Quick Check

Does your database look like this? If not, try the steps again.

First Name	Last Name	M/F	Grade	Hobby	Career Goal
Rina	Chang	F	5	swimming	firefighter
Pat	Jenkins	M	5	karate	writer
Flora	Mendez	F	5	painting	teacher
Jon	Nolan	M	5	baseball	hockey player

Jake's Ergonomics Tip

If you have a wrist rest, use it only when you take a break. Never rest your wrists or arms on it when you are typing.

AppleWorks

1. Select the list of steps under *Directions*.
2. Select the **Outline** menu and choose **Label Style**.
3. Then select **Numeric**.

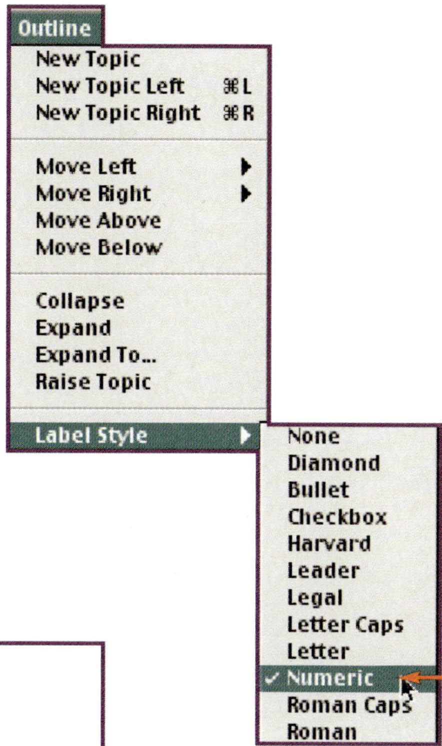

Select **Numeric**.

Quick Check

Do your directions look like this? If not, make your changes now.

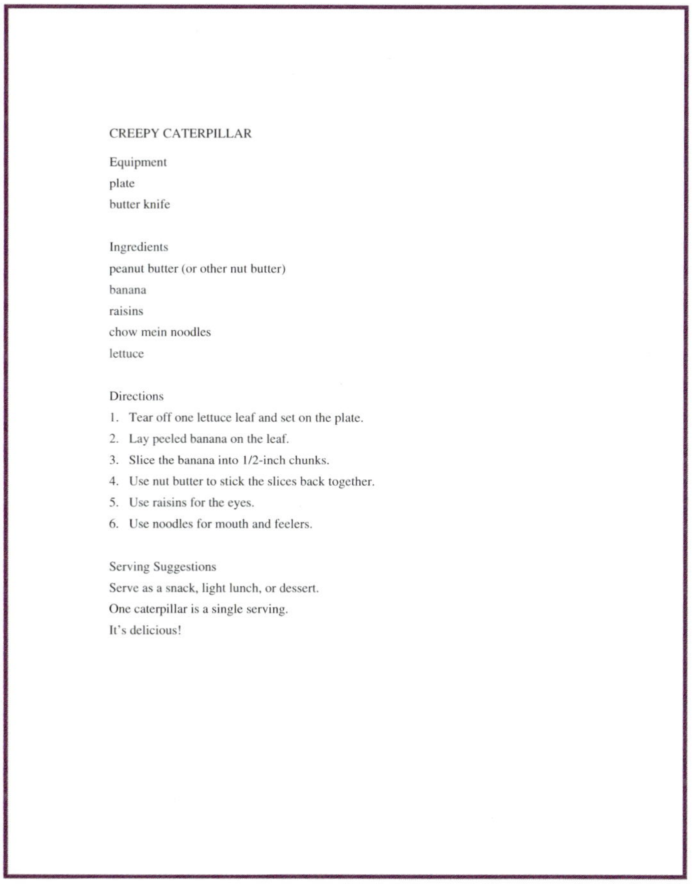

CREEPY CATERPILLAR

Equipment
plate
butter knife

Ingredients
peanut butter (or other nut butter)
banana
raisins
chow mein noodles
lettuce

Directions

1. Tear off one lettuce leaf and set on the plate.
2. Lay peeled banana on the leaf.
3. Slice the banana into 1/2-inch chunks.
4. Use nut butter to stick the slices back together.
5. Use raisins for the eyes.
6. Use noodles for mouth and feelers.

Serving Suggestions
Serve as a snack, light lunch, or dessert.
One caterpillar is a single serving.
It's delicious!

The fields in my database are* First Name, Last Name, M/F *(for male or female),* Grade, *and* Hobby. *There are four* records *in my database. Each record is for one student.

***Now let's improve my database by adding a new field called* Career Goal.**

Access

1. Choose **Design View** from the **View** menu.
2. Click in the row below the last field, which is ***Hobby***.
3. Type the new field name ***Career Goal***.
4. Save your file.

	Field Name	Data Type	Description
	First Name	Text	
	Last Name	Text	
	M/F	Text	
	Grade	Text	
	Hobby	Text	
▶	Career Goal	Text	

AppleWorks

1. Choose **Define Fields** from the **Layout** menu.
2. Type the new field name ***Career Goal*** in the **Field Name** box.
3. Click on **Create**.
4. Click on **Done**.
5. Save your file.

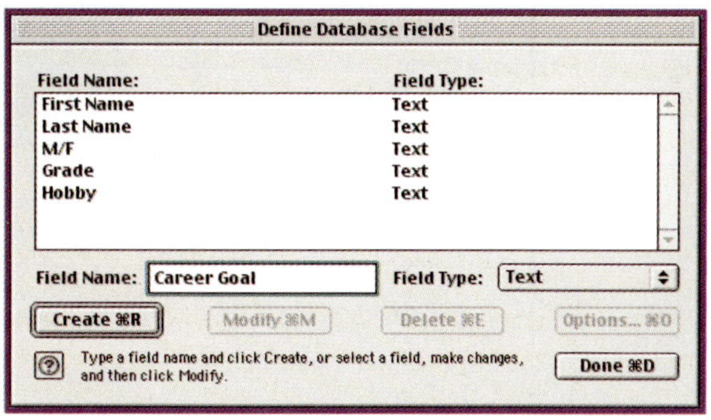

Access users should choose ***Datasheet View*** *from the* ***View*** *menu after adding the new field.*

PART 3

A Tasty List

Let's insert some bullets for the ingredients. That will make them stand out.

Word

1. Select the list of ingredients.
2. Select the **Format** menu and choose **Bullets and Numbering**.
3. Click on the **Bulleted** tab.
4. Click on the first box of bullets.
5. Click on **OK**.
6. Save your work.

AppleWorks

1. Select the list of ingredients.
2. Select the **Outline** menu and choose **Label Style**.
3. Then select **Bullet**.
4. Save your work.

Quick Check

Your list of ingredients should look like this.

Word

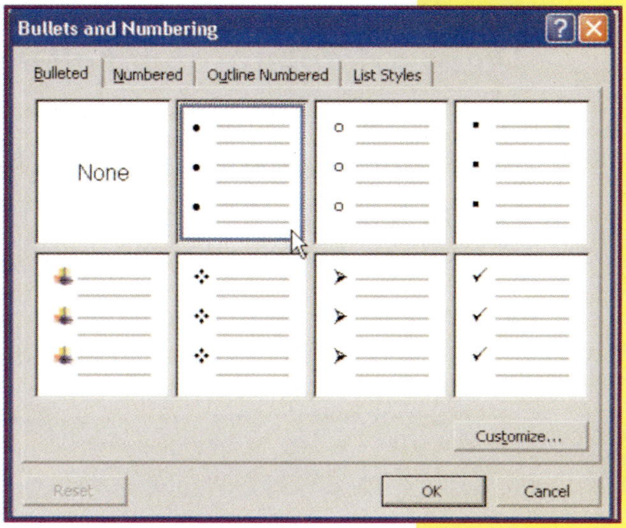

Select **Bullet**.

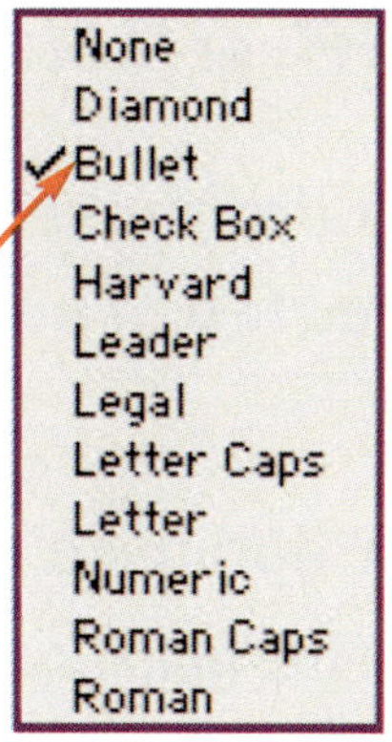

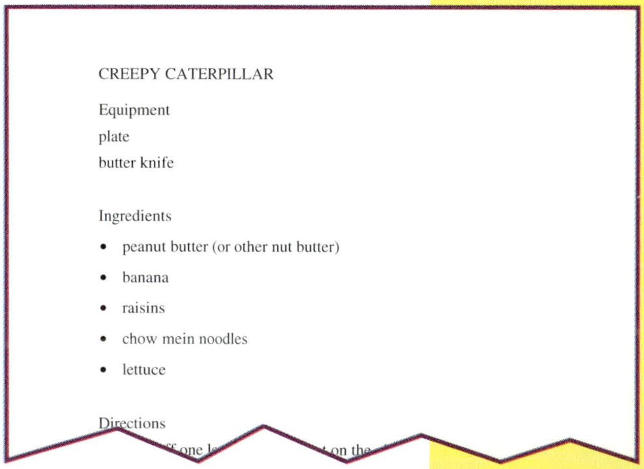
CREEPY CATERPILLAR

Equipment
plate
butter knife

Ingredients
- peanut butter (or other nut butter)
- banana
- raisins
- chow mein noodles
- lettuce

Directions

Project
17

Create a Student Profile Database

I keep a database about all my students. I keep track of their names and the grades they are in. But I am interested in more than just facts about each student. Each student is a person, with special interests and hobbies. I would like to add some of that information to my database. I could use your help!

PART 1

Up Close and Personal

Let's open my database and look at the fields that I have created. Then we will add a new field.

In Access, you must also open the table. Click on the icon next to the table named students.

1. Open your database program.
2. Open the file *students*.
3. Save the file as *students17*.

The* students17 *database should look like this.

students : Table

First Name	Last Name	M/F	Grade	Hobby
Rina	Chang	F	5	swimming
Pat	Jenkins	M	5	karate
Flora	Mendez	F	5	painting
Jon	Nolan	M	5	baseball

PART 4

Finishing Touches

You can make your recipe more interesting by using different words that have the same meaning. Replace the word* delicious *at the end of the recipe with another interesting word. Use the thesaurus in your word processing program to find synonyms, or words with the same meaning.

1. Select the word ***delicious***.

Word

2. Select the **Tools** menu.
3. Choose **Thesaurus**.
4. Read the definition of your word. Then read the list of words with the same meaning.
5. **Click** on the word that you want to use.
6. Click on **Replace**.
7. Save your work.

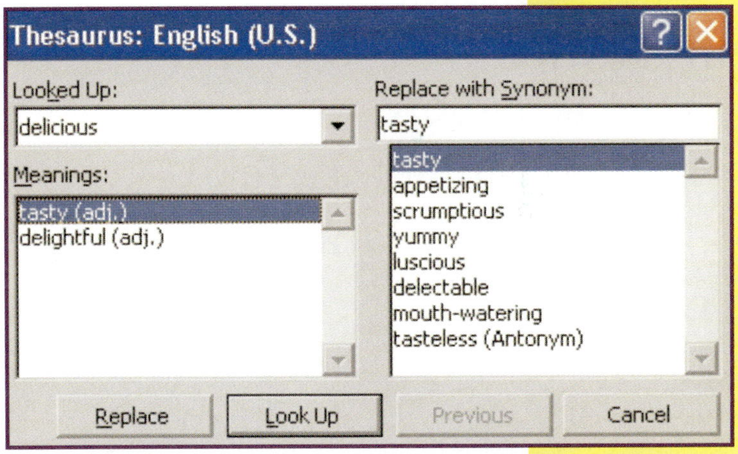

Jake's Ergonomics Tip

If you are right-handed, you keep the mouse on your right. If you are left-handed, you keep it on your left. As you work, make sure you are not leaning your whole body to that side. If you are leaning, straighten up and move the mouse nearer to the keyboard. Otherwise, you may strain the muscles in your side or back.

Project
17

Database

Student Profiles

In this project you will:

- Insert a field
- Add data
- Insert a record
- Delete a field
- Delete a record
- Move a field
- Sort data

Word Power

field

Layout menu

List layout

record

sort

Sort Ascending button

AppleWorks

2. Select the **Edit** menu in the toolbar. Choose **Writing Tools**.
3. Choose **Thesaurus**.
4. Read the definition of your word. Then read the list of words with the same meaning.
5. Select the word you want. Then click on **Insert**.
6. Click on **Done** to return to your document.
7. Save your work.

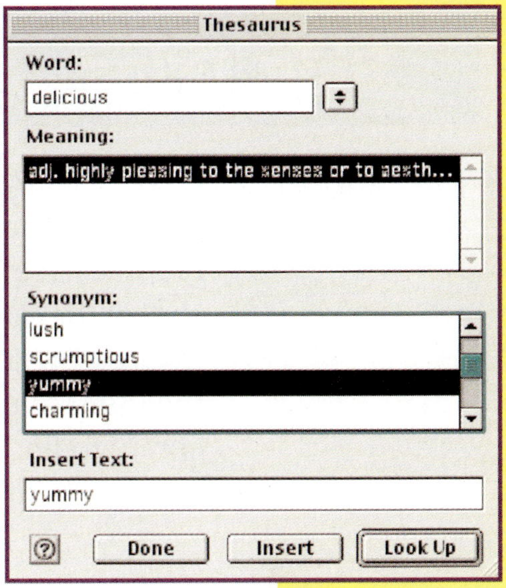

Thanks! My recipe looks great! Now, for the finishing touch, add a piece of clip art to make the recipe even more appealing.

Remember to save your work often! Click on the ***Save*** *button to save time!*

On Your Own

Change the bullets you used for your list of ingredients. Repeat the steps you followed for inserting the bullets, but this time choose a different style of bullets. You can also change the style of the numbers you used for your directions.

Side Trips with Blueberry and Jess

Social Studies

Research Modify the *states16* database to create a database that lists the geographical features of six states of your choice. Rename the fields with terms such as *lakes*, *rivers*, *mountains*, and *plants*. Use the Internet or books from your school library to find maps of each state. Save your database as *my states*.

Health

Record Modify the *states16* database to create a database of what you eat each day for a week. Include fields for the days of the week. Include records for breakfast, lunch, dinner, and snacks. Add data to the database each day. Save your database as *my meals*.

Bernie's Typing Activities

Open your word processor. Key the drill lines.

Review

all letters learned

1 cry the ask jet not file desk jar yield;
2 cry the ask jet not file desk jar yield;

double letters

3 off added fill letter jelly knee assist;
4 off added fill letter jelly knee assist;

one-hand words left hand

5 red after data fast feed radar tree area
6 red after data fast feed radar tree area

one-hand words right hand

7 hill join link hook lily only lion look;
8 hill join link hook lily only lion look;

balanced-hand words

9 aisle did field half island jay lend toe
10 aisle did field half island jay lend toe

left shift

11 Illinois; Indiana; Kansas; North Dakota;
12 Illinois; Indiana; Kansas; North Dakota;

phrases

13 it is the | he can | are not | she can | and the
14 it is the | he can | are not | she can | and the

Bernie's Typing Activities

Key each drill line twice; key each paragraph once.

Skill Building

space bar

1. Jacques may go to the mall with Max Cox.
2. Did she see Zelda set off down the road?

balanced-hand sentences

3. They kept the eight big bushels of corn.
4. Did she sign the forms for the city bus?
5. Hal and I may go to town for the social.

What Am I?

I was a gift to the United States from the people of France. I am a symbol of freedom. I am located in the New York Harbor.

I stand over 150 feet tall and weigh 450,000 pounds. I was the first thing many immigrants saw as they came to the United States. What am I?

Side Trips with Blueberry and Jess

Language Arts

Write What recipes can you make? Do you have a favorite recipe that uses bananas? Use your word processor to type a recipe. Number each step, and be sure to put the steps in order. BONUS: Make your recipe, and bring in the results to share with your classmates!

Health

Analyze Figure out how healthy your favorite recipe is. Look in a cookbook for information about the vitamins and other nutrients in each ingredient. Does your recipe help you get the vitamins you need every day? Use a word processor to write a short report about how your recipe helps you stay healthy. List the vitamins, setting them off with bullets.

AppleWorks

1. Choose **Find/Change** from the **Edit** menu.
2. Choose **Find/Change**.
3. In the **Find** box, type *New Hampshire*.
4. Click on **Find Next**.

New Hampshire *should be highlighted in the database.*

5. Close the **Find** box.
6. Use the **Tab** key to move to the *Capital* field.
7. What is the capital of New Hampshire? If you said Concord, you are right!

Repeat the steps above, but this time search for the words* red clover. *What state has red clover as its state flower?

Good work! You know your way around a database!

On Your Own

Add a new field labeled* State Bird *to the database. Use electronic reference tools, such as encyclopedia CD-ROMs or the Internet, to find this information for the database. Follow the steps you learned in this project to add a new field and insert data. Be sure to use a spelling checker!

Project
4

Word Processing

The Great Debate

In this project you will:

- Create a table
- Use the Copy and Paste commands
- Format a table

Word Power

cell

column

column heading

Copy button

Paste button

row

shading

table

PART 5

A Database Search

Now let's use the database to find information. We can search the database to find specific data. I want to know what the capital of New Hampshire is. Can you help?

Access

1. From the **Edit** menu, choose **Find**.
2. In the **Find What** field, type *New Hampshire*.
3. In the **Look In** box, click on the drop-down arrow and select *states:Table*.
4. Click on **Find Next**.

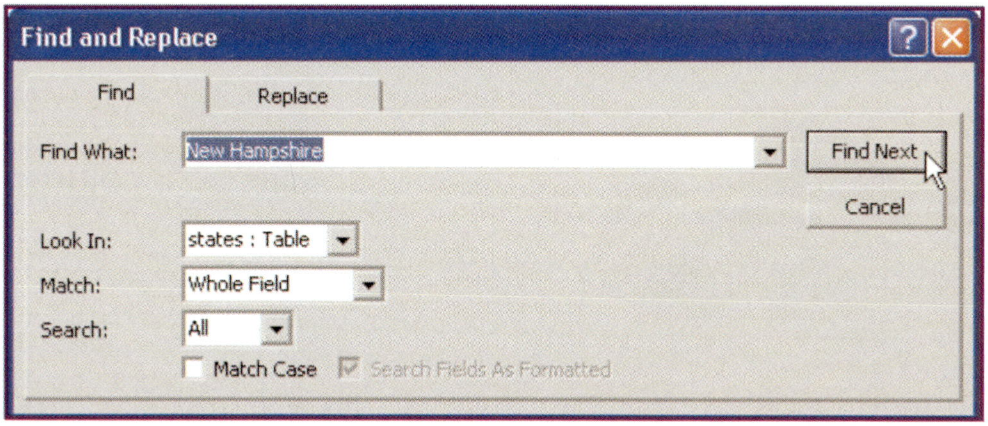

Jake's Ergonomics Tip

When you are typing, try to use the minimum amount of pressure necessary to tap the keys. The tendons from your fingers connect near your elbow, so tapping the keys too hard can lead to problems (pain and inflammation in your elbows).

Create a Table of Causes and Effects

I used the Time Machine to travel back in time to Boston, Massachusetts, in 1775. I wanted to find out the reasons, or causes, that led the colonists to go to war with England. I arrived in the middle of a lively meeting of local Patriots. Now I want to summarize what I heard by creating a table that lists the causes and effects of actions taken by the British and the Americans. Will you help me? I knew you would!

PART 1

Table Talk

First we need to open the file. You know how to do that by now. Then we will insert a table. How many columns do you think a cause-and-effect table will have? Of course, it will have two! One column will list causes and the other column will list effects.

1. Open the file named *causes*.
2. Place your cursor at the end of the file.
3. Tap **Enter**.
4. Save the file as *causes4*.

PART 4

One Less Field

You are doing a super job! But I am not sure that I need the* Statehood *field after all. Let's delete that one.

Access

1. Click on the field name *Statehood*.
2. From the **Edit** menu, choose **Delete Column**.
3. Save the file again.

AppleWorks

1. Choose **Define Fields** from the **Layout** menu.
2. Select the field name *Statehood*.
3. Click on the **Delete** button.
4. Save the file.

Quick Check

Great! Your database should look like this. If it does not, make the changes now.

State	Capital	State Flower	State Nickname
Connecticut	Hartford	mountain laurel	Constitution State
Rhode Island	Providence	violet	Ocean State
Massachusetts	Boston	mayflower	Bay State
New Hampshire	Concord	purple lilac	Granite State
Vermont	Montpelier	red clover	The Green Mountain State
Maine	Augusta	Eastern white pine cone and tassel	The Pine Tree State

Now let's insert the table.

Word

5 Choose **Insert** from the **Table** menu, then choose **Table**.

AppleWorks

5 Choose **Insert Table** from the **Table** menu.

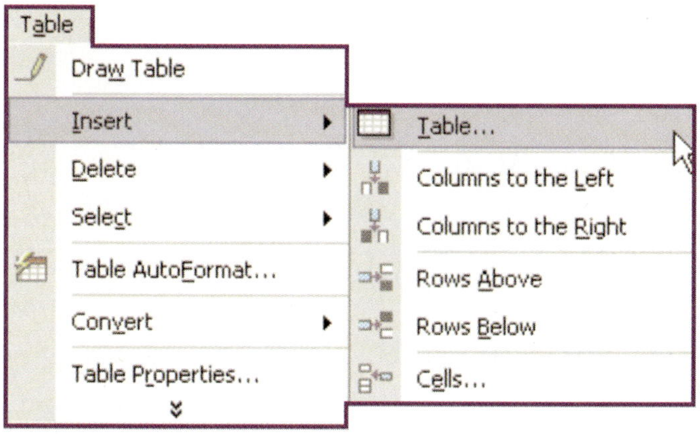

In the dialog box, type in the number of columns and rows you want in your table. You will need two columns and six rows.

6 Type *2* for the number of columns.

7 Type *6* for the number of rows.

AppleWorks

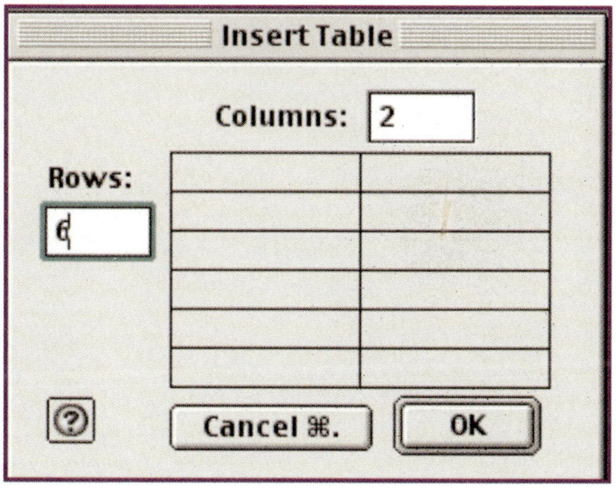

Word

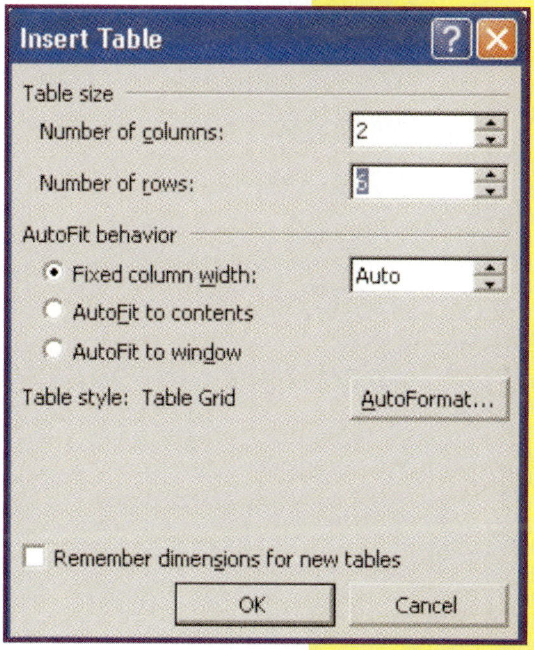

After looking at my database, I have decided to change the field* Nickname *to* State Nickname. *Let's do it.

Access

1. Select the *Nickname* column.
2. Choose **Rename Column** from the **Format** menu.
3. Type *State* before *Nickname*.
4. Save the file.

AppleWorks

1. Choose **Define Fields** from the **Layout** menu.
2. Click on the field *Nickname*.
3. Type *State* before *Nickname*.
4. Click on **Modify**.
5. Click on **Done**.
6. Save the file again.

Great! Now let's add the data for the* State Nickname *field.

1. Enter the data below into the *State Nickname* field.
2. Save the file.

State	State Nickname
Connecticut	Constitution State
Rhode Island	Ocean State
Massachusetts	Bay State
New Hampshire	Granite State
Vermont	The Green Mountain State
Maine	The Pine Tree State

Super! Your database should look like this.

State	Capital	State Flower	State Nickname	Statehood
Connecticut	Hartford	mountain laurel	Constitution State	
Rhode Island	Providence	violet	Ocean State	
Massachusetts	Boston	mayflower	Bay State	
New Hampshire	Concord	purple lilac	Granite State	
Vermont	Montpelier	red clover	The Green Mountain State	
Maine	Augusta	Eastern white pine cone and tassel	The Pine Tree State	

You should have a blank table in your file now. Each box in the table is called a cell.

Now let's add column headings.

8. Type the word ***Causes*** in the left column. Type the word ***Effects*** in the right column.
9. Save your changes.

columns

rows

Causes	Effects

PART 2

Fill in the Blanks

The information about causes and effects is in my notes. Each speaker gives one cause, or reason, that shows why he is angry with England. Then the speaker gives an effect, or result, of the cause. Use your arrow keys or the mouse to move the cursor to the beginning of the file. We will copy the sentence that gives a cause and paste it into the first row under Causes. Are you with me? Good!

PART 3

What's in a Name?

I have some other interesting facts to add. Did you know that each state has a nickname? Each state joined the Union in a specific year. Let's create two new fields for this information.

PowerPoint users should choose ***Datasheet View*** *from the* ***View*** *menu after adding the new field.*

Access

1. Choose **Design View** from the **View** menu.
2. Click on the next empty row in the table.
3. Type the new field name *Nickname*.
4. Save the file.

AppleWorks

1. Choose **Define Fields** from the **Layout** menu.
2. Type the new field name *Nickname*.
3. Click on the **Create** button.
4. Click on the **Done** button.
5. Save the file.

Now add another field named **Statehood**. ***Follow the same steps you used to add the field*** **Nickname** ***to the database.***

Quick Check

Your database should look like this now. It should have five fields.

The new fields *Nickname* and *Statehood* are added here.

State	Capital	State Flower	Nickname	Statehood
Connecticut	Hartford	mountain laurel		
Rhode Island	Providence	violet		
Massachusetts	Boston	mayflower		
New Hampshire	Concord	purple lilac		
Vermont	Montpelier	red clover		
Maine	Augusta	Eastern white pine cone and tassel		

1. Select the first sentence under Speaker 1.
2. Choose **Copy** from the **Edit** menu.
3. Place your cursor in the first cell under ***Causes***.
4. Choose **Paste** from the **Edit** menu.

Causes	Effects
We elected a legislature, but the governor appointed by the king can veto any laws it passes.	

***That is all there is to it! Now we will copy and paste the second sentence under Speaker 1. This time, we will paste it under* Effects.**

5. Select the second sentence under Speaker 1.
6. Choose **Copy** from the **Edit** menu.
7. Place your cursor in the first cell under ***Effects***.
8. Choose **Paste** from the **Edit** menu.

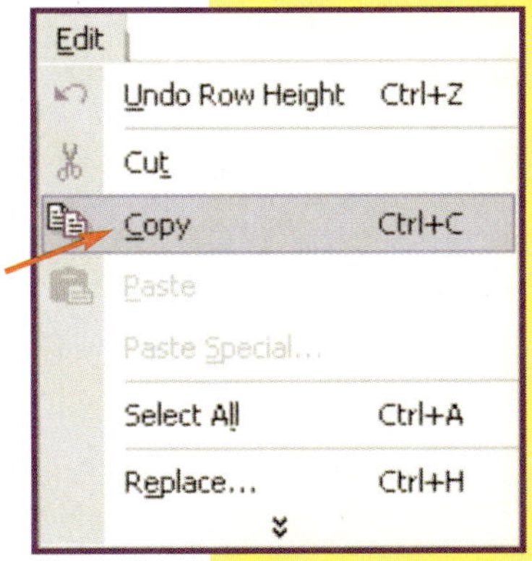

Choose **Copy** from the **Edit** menu.

Quick Check

Your table should look like this.

Causes	Effects
We elected a legislature, but the governor appointed by the king can veto any laws it passes.	This shows us that England does not respect our rights!

Way to go! Now that you have created a new field called* State Flower, *let's fill in the data.

1. Use the data from my notepad to enter the state flowers for each state.

State	State Flower
Connecticut	mountain laurel
Rhode Island	violet
Massachusetts	mayflower
New Hampshire	purple lilac
Vermont	red clover
Maine	Eastern white pine cone and tassel

*Some words are capitalized. Use the **Shift** key to type the capital letters.*

If a name is too long for the column, click on the line between the two columns and drag the pointer to make the column wider.

2. Use the spelling checker to check your work.
3. Save the file.

State Flower
mountain laurel
violet
mayflower

The pointer should look like this to change the width of the column.

Quick Check

Terrific! The database should now look like this. If it does not, make the changes now.

State	Capital	State Flower
Connecticut	Hartford	mountain laurel
Rhode Island	Providence	violet
Massachusetts	Boston	mayflower
New Hampshire	Concord	purple lilac
Vermont	Montpelier	red clover
Maine	Augusta	Eastern white pine cone and tassel

Use the Copy and Paste buttons to fill in the next row.

9. Select the first sentence under Speaker 2.
10. Click on the **Copy** button.
11. Place your cursor in the next empty cell under *Causes*.
12. Click on the **Paste** button.
13. Save your work.

That was easy! Now copy and paste the second sentence under Speaker 2 into the next cell under* Effects. *When you copy and paste the sentences, you do not have to copy all the sentences. Just focus on the causes and effects.

Quick Check

Your table should look like this. If it does not, go back and make any changes.

Causes	Effects
We elected a legislature, but the governor appointed by the king can veto any laws it passes.	This shows us that England does not respect our rights!
England has forced us to agree not to manufacture goods.	This means that we cannot compete with British products.

Continue to fill out the table. Remember, choose only the most important sentence to paste in your chart. Your table may look different from mine.

PART 2

A Field of Flowers

***Now let's begin to add data to the database. I want to add a new field called* State Flower.**

PowerPoint users should choose **Datasheet View** from the **View** menu after adding the new field.

Access

1. Choose **Design View** from the **View** menu.
2. Click on the next empty row in the table.
3. Type the new field name *State Flower*.
4. Choose **Datasheet View** from the **View** menu.
5. Save the file.

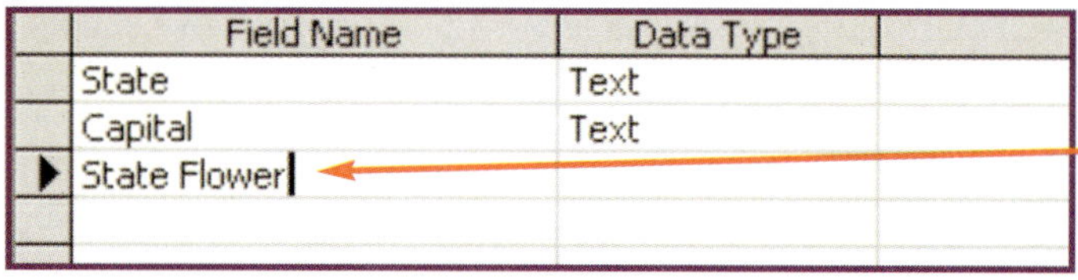

Field Name	Data Type	
State	Text	
Capital	Text	
State Flower		

Add a new field called *State Flower*.

AppleWorks

1. Choose **Define Fields** from the **Layout** menu.
2. Type the new field name *State Flower*.
3. Click on the **Create** button.
4. Click on the **Done** button.
5. Save the file.

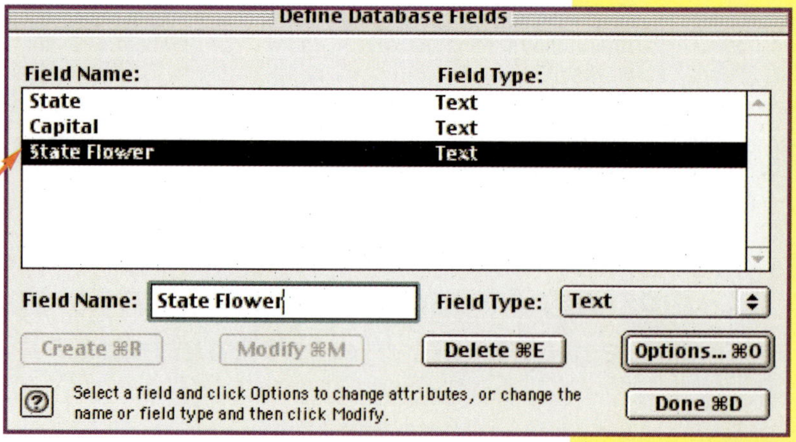

Add a new field called *State Flower*.

PART 3

Heading for Shade

This is a great cause-and-effect table. Now let's make the column headings stand out. This is what we will do:

- Center the column headings
- Make them bold
- Apply shading to them

Complete the steps below! It will be fun!

1. Select each column heading.
2. Click on the **Center** button on the toolbar. 
3. Click on the **Bold** button on the toolbar.

Causes	**Effects**
We elected a legislature, but the governor appointed by the king can veto any laws it passes.	This shows us that England does not respect our rights!

Both column headings should be centered in each column and in bold text.

Jake's Ergonomics Tip

You have done a lot. Try to relax now. Roll your shoulders around slowly in a big circle going backward. Do this four times. Then circle your shoulders forward. There, now you should be feeling a lot better!

The states database should look like this.

Fields

Records

	State	Capital
	Connecticut	Hartford
	Rhode Island	Providence
	Massachusetts	Boston
	New Hampshire	Concord
	Vermont	Montpelier
	Maine	Augusta
▶		

A database consists of fields and records. The fields in the database are the different categories. The fields labeled **State** ***and*** **Capital** ***are shown in the top row of the database. There are six records in this database. Each record contains the data for one state.***

You can move around in a database by using the Tab key or the arrow keys. Click on the state name **Connecticut.** ***Tap the Tab key to move to the next field. Hartford is the capital of Connecticut. Move to the sixth record in the database. What is the name of the state in this record? If you said Maine, you are correct! Move to the field that shows the capital of New Hampshire. What is it?***

In AppleWorks, you can move from record to record by clicking on the pages of the Record book. To move to a record, click on the Record page.

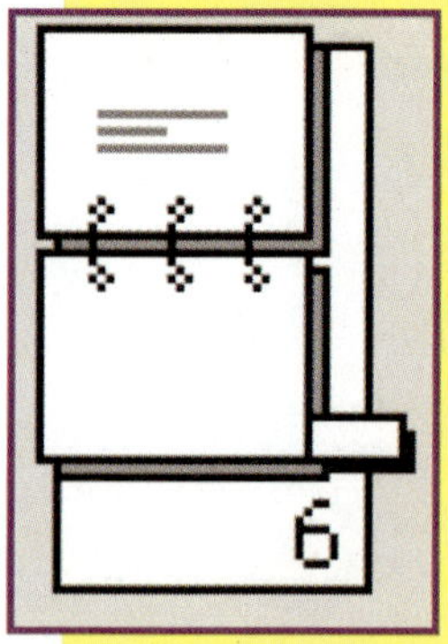

Now let's add shading to the headings.

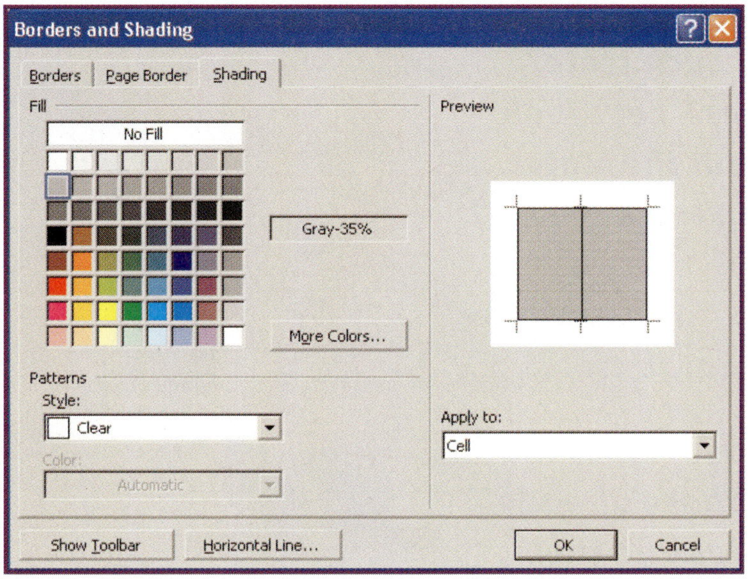

Word

4. Select the column headings ***Causes*** and ***Effects*** if necessary.
5. Choose **Borders and Shading** from the **Format** menu.
6. Click on the **Shading** tab.
7. Select a shade of green.
8. Click **OK**.
9. Save your work.

AppleWorks

4. Select the column headings ***Causes*** and ***Effects*** if necessary.
5. Choose **Show Accents** from the **Window** menu. Make sure the **Fill** box is selected.
6. Select a shade of green.
7. Save your work.

Project 16

Add to a Database About the States

Do you know the names of all fifty states in the United States? What is the capital of each state? What are the states' nicknames? Let's look for some interesting facts about the states. We can use a database to keep track of what we learn about each state. A database organizes information, or data. As we gather data, we can enter it into the database.

I have started a database that includes the six New England states. The database already includes the names of the states and their capitals. I need your help to complete the file. Are you ready? Let's go!

PART 1

Great States

Let's start by opening the database. If you are using Microsoft Access, your teacher will tell you which file to open.

1. Open your database program.
2. Open the file *states*.
3. Save the file as *states16*.

Quick Check

Have you:

- Centered the text in the column headings?
- Boldfaced the words?
- Applied shading to the column headings?

Your table should look like this.

Causes	Effects
We elected a legislature, but the governor appointed by the king can veto any laws it passes.	This shows us that England does not respect our rights!
England has forced us to agree not to manufacture goods.	This means that we cannot compete with British products.
Britain borrowed money to fight the French and Indian War that ended in 1763.	Now the leaders over there want us to pay for the money they borrowed.
Great Britain passed the intolerable Stamp Act.	Suddenly Americans had to buy stamps for everything from deeds and mortgages to licenses and newspapers.
We have no representatives in the English Parliament.	This is taxation without representation.

On Your Own

Make some more changes to your table. Use one style for the sentences that name causes and a different style for the sentences that name effects. Use the Bold, Italic, or Underline buttons on the toolbar to change the style of the sentences. Which way looks best to you?

Project 16

Database

Across America

In this project you will:

- Use a database
- Add data
- Insert, modify, and delete a field
- Search for data

Word Power

data

database

field

record

search

Bernie's Typing Activities

Open your word processor.
Key the drill lines.

Reinforce: m, period, u, p, w, g

all letters learned

1 Jack ton heir safely done lack nick are;
2 Jack ton heir safely done lack nick are;

m emphasis

3 milk money | manmade marsh | James and Marie
4 milk money | manmade marsh | James and Marie

period emphasis

5 Mr. Mrs. Ms. N. Dak. a.m. misc. Inc. Jr.
6 Mr. Mrs. Ms. N. Dak. a.m. misc. Inc. Jr.

u emphasis

7 Ursula usually hurries to see us unload.
8 Ursula usually hurries to see us unload.

p emphasis

9 Pat and Paul put the puppy on the paper.
10 Pat and Paul put the puppy on the paper.

w emphasis

11 wayward westward whirlwind woodwind whew
12 wayward westward whirlwind woodwind whew

g emphasis

13 green garage | gas gauge | large eggs | go get
14 green garage | gas gauge | large eggs | go get

Side Trips with Blueberry and Jess

Language Arts

Create Imagine that you are going on a trip for five days. Create a spreadsheet to keep track of things you will spend your money on while you are traveling. For example, you will buy gas. You will buy food. You may go to a museum or an amusement park. Add column headings for things you will buy or spend money on. Use the days of the week for your row headings. Be sure to add a row that will show the total expenses.

Math

Calculate Design a spreadsheet that shows how many miles a day you walk. Find the average number of miles you walk in one week. Try changing the number of miles for a day or two in your spreadsheet and see how the changes affect the totals and the averages.

Side Trips with Blueberry and Jess

Art

Persuade Imagine that you are living during the time of the American Revolution. Create a poster on the computer that encourages others to support the war. Your poster should also tell people what they can do to show their support. Use bold, italic, and underlines. Center the most important sentences. Add clip art.

Language Arts

Persuade Imagine that you are speaking at a town meeting. You want to persuade your audience to go to war with England. Use the causes and effects to write a persuasive speech that will rally the colonists to your side. Type your speech on the computer. Find ways to make your speech more persuasive. You can ask a question and then answer it. You can repeat words. Practice giving your speech. Then deliver your speech to your classmates.

Bernie's Typing Activities

Key each drill line twice; key each paragraph once.

Reinforce: 6 & 2

1. On November 22, 1963, John Kennedy died.
2. I have 6 extra large sizes and 22 large.
3. March 6, April 26, and June 26 are open.
4. All 662 members attended the 2004 rally.
5. Kansas was admitted on January 29, 1861.

Who Am I?

I was born in the big woods of Wisconsin 1867. I have a sister whose name is Mary. When I was a baby we moved to Missouri and later on to Kansas.

My parents built a little house on the quiet prairie in Kansas. Later in life I wrote books. There was also a television series about my life. Who am I?

Project
5
Word Processing

Smile!

In this project you will:

- Use the thesaurus
- Use the Find/Change or Replace command
- Change the margins
- Set tabs
- Change fonts

Word Power

Find/Change

Replace

tab

Then center the column headings and make them bold. You can also change the font, font size, and color of the headings.

4. Save your work.

Quick Check

Good job! Your spreadsheet might look like this.

	A	B	C	D	E
1				Your name	
2			My Mileage Calculations: 1,200 miles from Cincinnati to Miami		
3					
4					
5		**Hours**	**Speed (m.p.h.)**	**Miles covered**	**How many days at this speed?**
6	What if we drive	6	65	390	3.08
7	What if we drive	6	60	360	3.33
8	What if we drive	6	55	330	3.64
9	What if we drive	6	50	300	4.00
10	What if we drive	6	45	270	4.44
11	Average	6	55	330	3.64

On Your Own

Use the Internet to find a map for Bernie's trip from Cincinnati to Miami. Go to a map-building Web site, such as www.mapquest.com. Type the name* Cincinnati, Ohio, *as the starting point and* Miami, Florida, *as the destination. You should see a map with a red line showing the route. Copy the map and paste it in your spreadsheet. Be sure to cite your source.

Project 5

Make an Invitation

Do you know what World Smile Day is? A man named Harvey Ball created the Smiley Face to make people feel happy. Then he decided to have a World Smile Day to remind people that they can make someone smile by doing an act of kindness. Our school is going to celebrate World Smile Day by having a party after school. Will you help me make an invitation? Making invitations on the computer is lots of fun!

PART 1

Party Words

I want my invitation to make everyone feel enthusiastic about the party. Using descriptive and colorful words will help. We can use the thesaurus. Let's go!

1. Open the file named *invitation*.
2. Choose **Save As** from the **File** menu.
3. Name the file *invitation5*.
4. Save the file.

Quick Check

Excellent! That was hard work! Does your spreadsheet look like this? If not, try the steps again.

	A	B	C	D	E
1				Your name	
2			My Mileage Calculations: 1,200 miles from Cincinnati to Miami		
3					
4					
5		Hours	Speed (m.p.h.)	Miles covered	How many days at this speed?
6	What if we drive	6	65	390	3.08
7	What if we drive	6	60	360	3.33
8	What if we drive	6	55	330	3.64
9	What if we drive	6	50	300	4.00
10	What if we drive	6	45	270	4.44
11	Average	6	55	330	3.64
12					

PART 6

Our Final Destination

This is a spreadsheet to be proud of! Let's finish it up by adding borders and shading. We will also add a map!

1. Select cells A5:E11.

Excel

2. Click on the drop-down menu of the **Borders** button.
3. Click on the **All Borders** option.

AppleWorks

2. Click on the **Outline Border**, **Left Border**, **Top Border**, **Right Border**, and **Bottom Border** buttons.

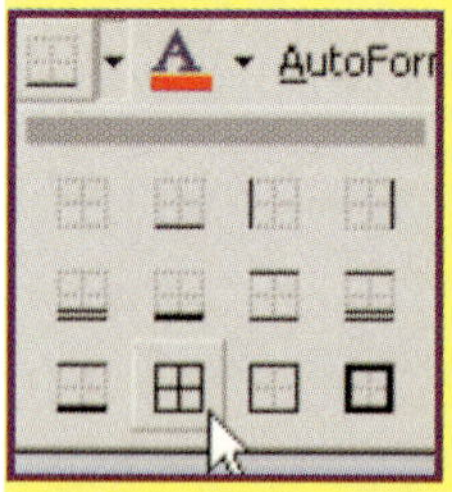

Now add shading to the column headings and Averages row. In Excel, click on the Fill Color tool. In AppleWorks, click on the Color palette button.

Let's use another word for **smile** *in the list of three items with exclamation points.*

5. Double-click on the word *Smile*.

Word

6. Choose **Language** from the **Tools** menu, and then select **Thesaurus**.

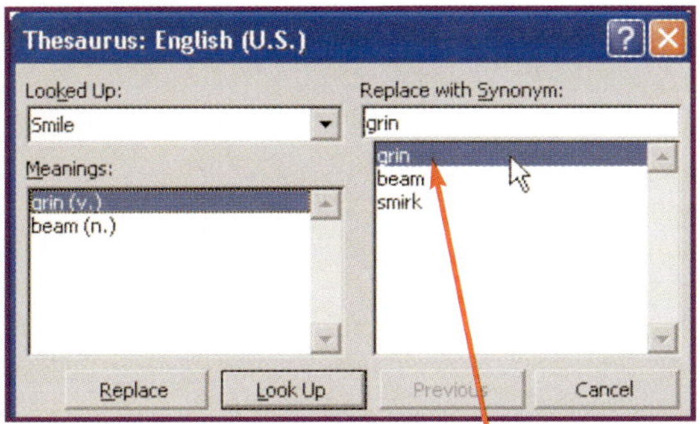

Choose *grin* from the list.

AppleWorks

6. Choose **Writing Tools** from the **Edit** menu, and then select **Thesaurus**.

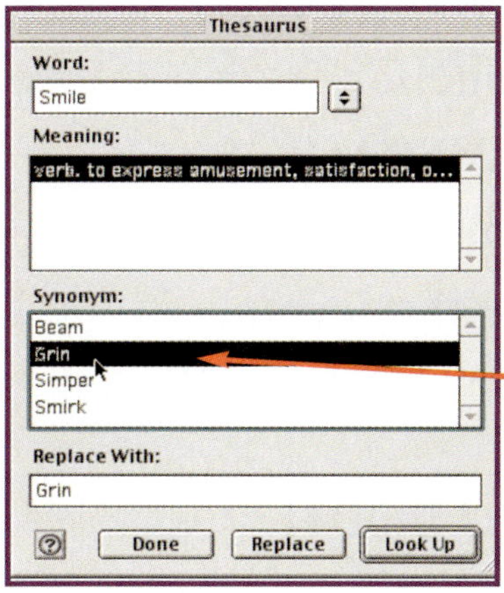

Choose *grin* from the list.

7. Read the list of words and click on *grin*.
8. Click on **Replace**.
9. Change the *g* to a capital letter.

Now replace the word **happy** *in the last sentence.*

10. Double-click on *happy*.
11. Open the thesaurus.
12. Click on *joyful*.
13. Click on **Replace**.
14. Save your work.

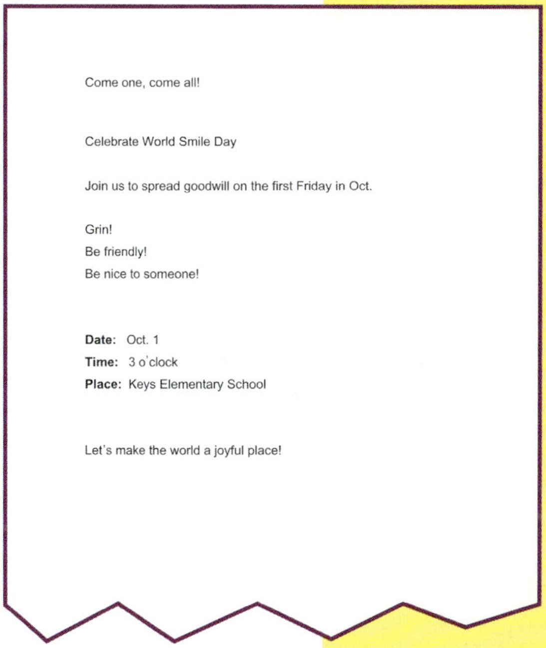

Come one, come all!

Celebrate World Smile Day

Join us to spread goodwill on the first Friday in Oct.

Grin!
Be friendly!
Be nice to someone!

Date: Oct. 1
Time: 3 o'clock
Place: Keys Elementary School

Let's make the world a joyful place!

PART 5

The End of the Road

The end of our work is in sight! The next step is to calculate how many miles we can drive per day at the average speed.

Excel

1. Click on cell D11.
2. Choose **Function** from the **Insert** menu.
3. Click on **AVERAGE**.
4. Click on **OK**.
5. Make sure the formula in the **Number 1** box shows D6:D10, and click on **OK**.

AppleWorks

1. Select cells D6:D11.
2. Choose **Auto Average** from the **Calculate** menu.

Did you get the number 330? That is the number of miles we can drive per day at the average speed.

If we can drive 330 miles per day, how many days will it take to drive 1,200 miles?

1. Click on cell E11.
2. Type *=PRODUCT(1200/D11)*.
3. Tap **Enter**.
4. Save your file.

PART 2

A Global Change

World Smile Day is held on the first Friday in October. I abbreviated the month instead of spelling out October. I want to spell it out. We can let the computer do it for us. Let's do it now!

Put your cursor at the beginning of the document.

1. Choose **Replace** or **Find/Change** from the **Edit** menu.
2. Type in ***Oct.*** in the **Find what** or **Find** box. Be sure to type the period!
3. Type ***October*** in the **Replace with** or **Change** box.
4. Click on **Replace All** or **Change All**.
5. Click on **OK** when the two replacements have been made.
6. Save your work.

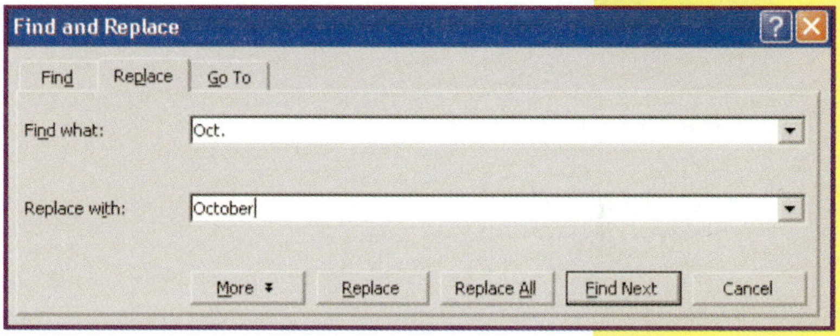

Quick Check

Super! Does your invitation look like this? Make any changes now, if necessary.

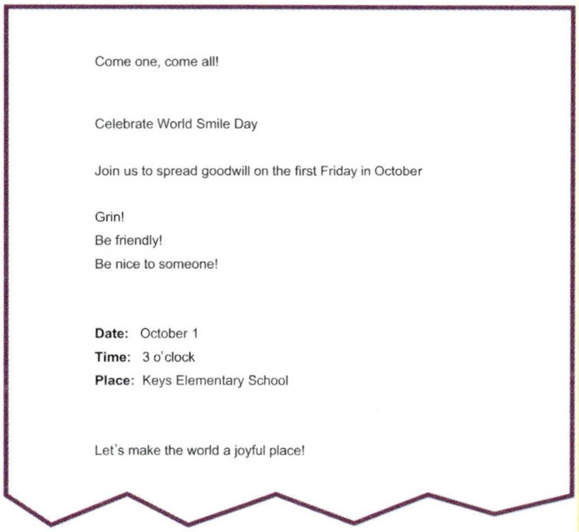
Come one, come all!

Celebrate World Smile Day

Join us to spread goodwill on the first Friday in October

Grin!
Be friendly!
Be nice to someone!

Date: October 1
Time: 3 o'clock
Place: Keys Elementary School

Let's make the world a joyful place!

You want to average all the speeds in column C—cells C6, C7, C8, C9, and C10.

8. Make sure the formula in the **Number 1** box shows **C6:C10**.

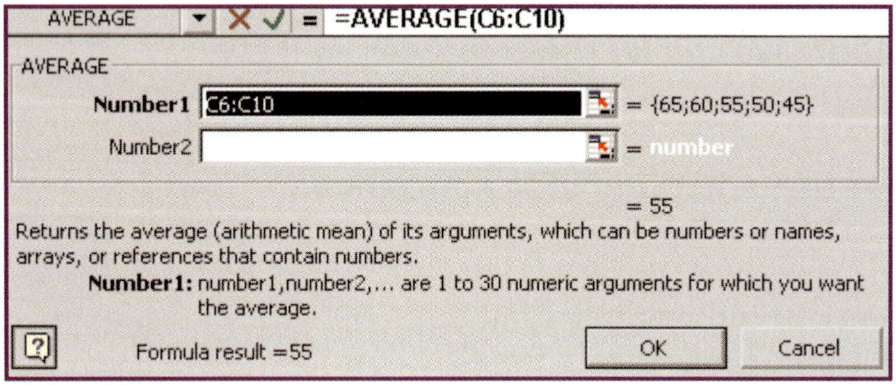

9. Click **OK**.

Cell C11 should show 55, which is the average of 65, 60, 55, 50, and 45.

10. Save your file.

AppleWorks

4. Select cells C6:C11.
5. Choose **Auto Average** from the **Calculate** menu.
6. Save the file.

Quick Check

Your spreadsheet should look like this. If not, try the steps again.

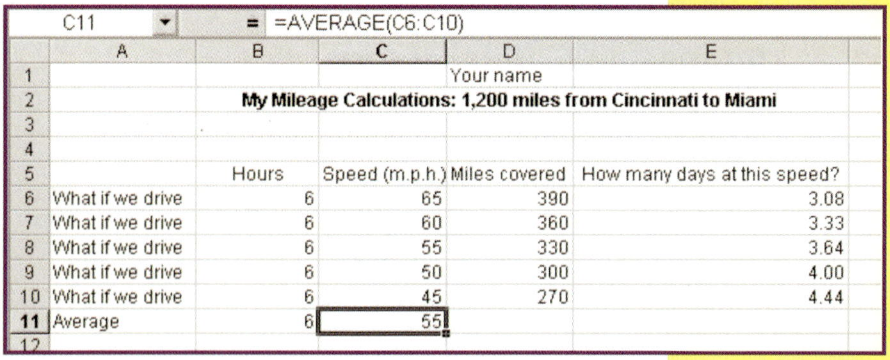

C11 = =AVERAGE(C6:C10)

	A	B	C	D	E
1				Your name	
2		My Mileage Calculations: 1,200 miles from Cincinnati to Miami			
3					
4					
5		Hours	Speed (m.p.h.)	Miles covered	How many days at this speed?
6	What if we drive	6	65	390	3.08
7	What if we drive	6	60	360	3.33
8	What if we drive	6	55	330	3.64
9	What if we drive	6	50	300	4.00
10	What if we drive	6	45	270	4.44
11	Average	6	55		
12					

PART 3

An Inviting Design

This invitation is really shaping up. Now that we have the words, we need a good design. Our invitation should have a good balance between words and space. Let's begin by setting wide margins.

Word

1. Choose **Page Setup** from the **File** menu.

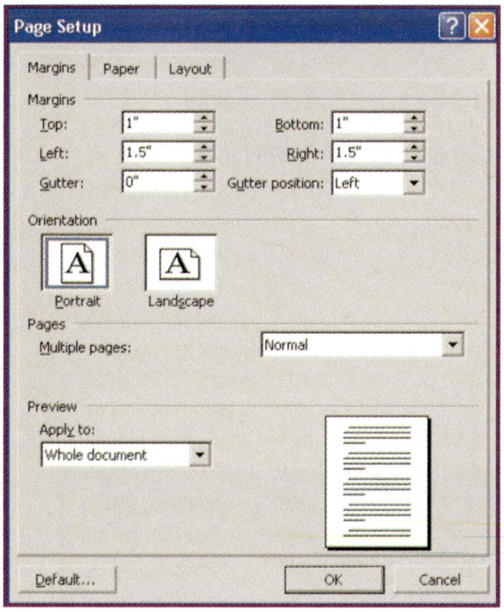

AppleWorks

1. Choose **Document** from the **Format** menu.

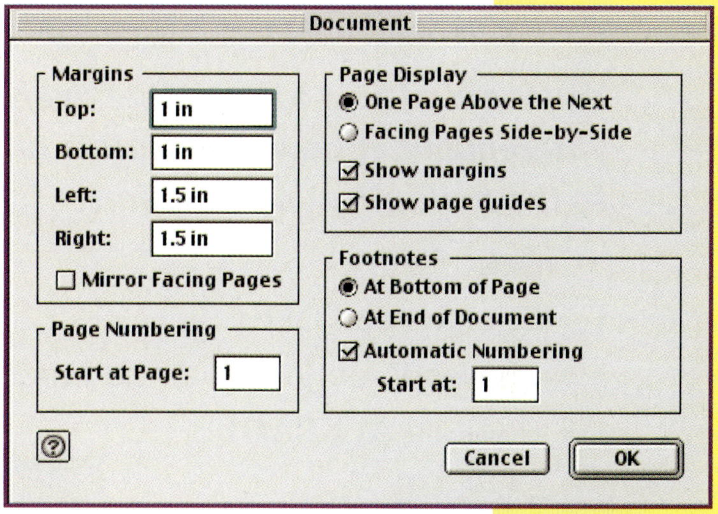

2. Set the top and bottom margins at 1 inch.
3. Set the left and right margins at 1.5 inches.

Let's also make sure that our page is set up in Portrait orientation. If you are using AppleWorks, choose Page Setup from the File menu to check the page orientation.

4. Click on **OK**.

You can tap the ***Tab*** *key or use your mouse to move to each box.*

PART 4

The Average Speed

You are doing such a good job! Of course, nobody can drive at the same speed for six whole hours. Our real speed will probably be an average of all of the speeds in column C. Let's figure out the average speed. We need to add a new row for this information.

1. Click on cell **A11**.
2. Type *Average*.
3. Click on cell **B11** and type the number *6*.

You learned how to calculate averages in Project 13. Do you remember how to calculate an average? It is similar to the multiplication function.

Excel

4. Click on cell C11.
5. Choose **Function** from the **Insert** menu.
6. Click on **AVERAGE**.
7. Click **OK**.

Click on **AVERAGE**.

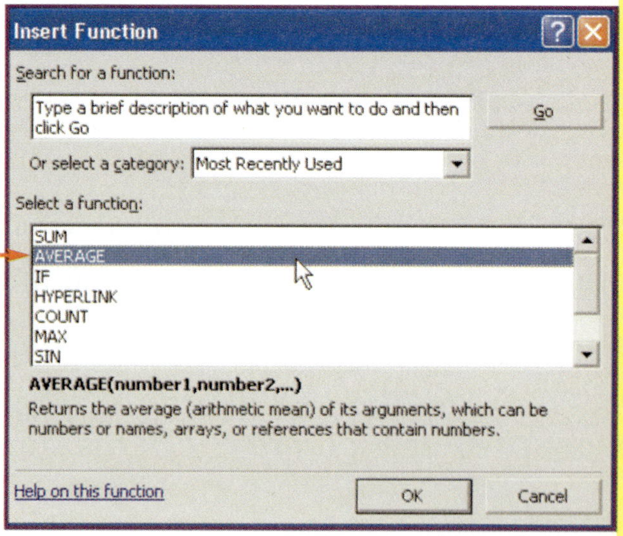

Now let's center the first three lines.

5. Place your cursor at the beginning of the first line.
6. Click and drag to select the first three lines.
7. Click on the **Center** button on the toolbar.
8. Save your work.

Come one, come all!

Celebrate World Smile Day

Join us to spread goodwill on the first Friday in October

Grin!
Be friendly!
Be nice to someone!

Date: October 1
Time: 3 o'clock
Place: Keys Elementary School

Let's make the world a joyful place!

Jake's Ergonomics Tip

When you key, keep your fingers curved and upright over the home row keys. Keep your wrists low but not touching the keyboard. Lightly tap each key with the tip of your finger, snapping the fingertip toward the palm of your hand. Your hands and arms won't be as tired if you follow these simple directions.

Let's go ahead and figure out how many days it will take if we drive at the other speeds listed in column C.

4. Click on cell E7.
5. Type =*PRODUCT(1200/D7)*.
6. Tap **Enter**.
7. Click on cell E8.
8. Type =*PRODUCT(1200/D8)*.
9. Tap **Enter**.

You can do the last two cells on your own. You know how!

10. Save the file again.

*To check the formulas in each cell of column **E**, put your pointer on a cell. Look in the formula bar for the formula.*

Quick Check

Does your spreadsheet look like this? If not, try the steps again.

	A	B	C	D	E
1				Your name	
2			**My Mileage Calculations: 1,200 miles from Cincinnati to Miami**		
3					
4					
5		Hours	Speed (m.p.h.)	Miles covered	How many days at this speed?
6	What if we drive	6	65	390	3.08
7	What if we drive	6	60	360	3.33
8	What if we drive	6	55	330	3.64
9	What if we drive	6	50	300	4.00
10	What if we drive	6	45	270	4.44
11					

Jake's Ergonomics Tip

Arrange your monitor so you can see it easily and maintain good posture. Position it directly in front of you so you do not have to turn your head frequently.

PART 4

Tabs Rule!

The lines that give the information about the date, time, and place look good, but they can look even better. I want to indent these lines. We can set tabs in the ruler to do this.

1. Place your cursor in front of the word ***Date***.
2. Click on the 1-inch marker on the ruler to set a tab.
3. Strike the **Tab** key.

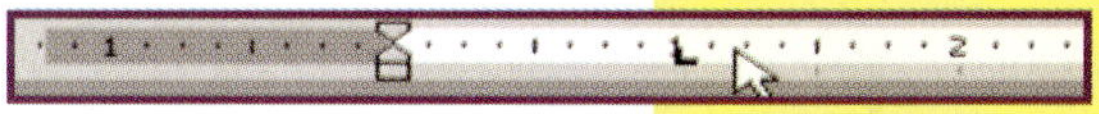

4. Place your cursor before the word ***Time***.
5. Then repeat steps 2 and 3.
6. Place your cursor before the word ***Place***.
7. Then repeat the steps.

Good job! If you want to clear, or remove, the tab stop, just drag it off the ruler.

Now let's set tabs for the three lines beginning with Grin.

8. Select the word ***Grin!*** and set a tab at 1.5 inches.
9. Select the line ***Be friendly!*** and set a tab at 2 inches.
10. Select the line ***Be nice to someone!*** and set a tab at 3 inches.
11. Save your work.

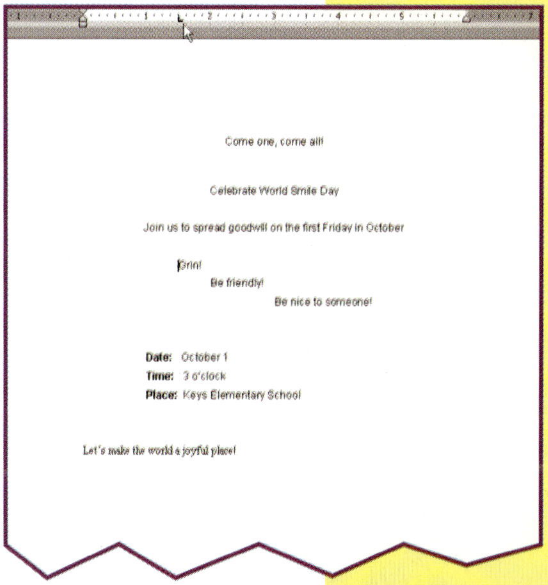

Quick Check

Super! The invitation should look like this. If it does not, make the changes now.

PART 3

Are We There Yet?

Now I know how many miles we can travel at each speed. So, how many days will it take us to travel 1,200 miles? We need to divide the total distance (1,200 miles) by the number of miles covered in one day.

1. Click on cell E6.

We need to type a division formula. The symbol for divide is a slash (/). We repeat the same steps we took for multiplication, but this time we use the slash symbol instead of an asterisk in our formula. Are you ready?

Type the number 1200 without a comma.

2. Type *=PRODUCT(1200/D6).*

The formula bar at the top of the screen should read: =PRODUCT(1200/D6).

3. Tap **Enter**.

E6 = =PRODUCT(1200/D6)

	A	B	C	D	E
1				Your name	
2		**My Mileage Calculations: 1,200 miles from Cincinnati to Miami**			
3					
4					
5		Hours	Speed (m.p.h.)	Miles covered	How many days at this speed?
6	What if we drive	6	65	390	3.08
7	What if we drive	6	60	360	
8	What if we drive	6	55	330	
9	What if we drive	6	50	300	
10	What if we drive	6	45	270	
11					

The formula is displayed in the formula bar.

Did you get 3.08 as your answer? It will take a little more than three days to get from Cincinnati to Miami if we drive 6 hours a day at 65 miles per hour.

PART 5

Playful Fonts

Some fonts are elegant or serious. Other fonts have a playful look. What font should we use for our invitation? Let's choose a font and font sizes to make certain words and phrases stand out.

1. Select the first line and change the font size to 24 points.
2. Select the words ***Celebrate World Smile Day.***
3. Click on the **Font** box and choose an interesting font.
4. Click on the **Font Size** box and choose 28.
5. Select the third line and change the font size to 24 points.
6. Select the last sentence, ***Let's make the world a joyful place!***
7. Click on the **Font Size** box and choose 22.
8. Click on the **Center** button on the toolbar.

Now put some of the text in color. The choice is yours!

9. Save your work.

There is one thing missing from the invitation—a Smiley Face! You can find a Smiley Face almost anywhere, so search for one on the Internet or insert a piece of clip art.

Now let's use the formula to calculate the mileage for each of the speeds in column C.

4. Click on cell D7.
5. Type *=PRODUCT(B7*C7).*
6. Tap **Enter**.
7. Click on cell D8.
8. Type *=PRODUCT(B8*C8).*
9. Tap **Enter**.
10. Click on cell D9.
11. Type *=PRODUCT(B9*C9).*
12. Tap **Enter**.
13. Click on cell D10.
14. Type *=PRODUCT(B10*C10).*
15. Tap **Enter**.
16. Save your work.

Good work! You have figured out how many miles my family could drive each day at different speeds.

Quick Check

Your spreadsheet should look like this. If it does not, try the steps again.

	A	B	C	D	E
1				Your name	
2		**My Mileage Calculations: 1,200 miles from Cincinnati to Miami**			
3					
4					
5		Hours	Speed (m.p.h.)	Miles covered	How many days at this speed?
6	What if we drive	6	65	390	
7	What if we drive	6	60	360	
8	What if we drive	6	55	330	
9	What if we drive	6	50	300	
10	What if we drive	6	45	270	

Quick Check

Does your invitation look something like this? If not, make your changes now.

Come one, come all!

Celebrate World Smile Day

Join us to spread goodwill on the first

Friday in October

Grin!

Be friendly!

Be nice to someone!

Date: October 1
Time: 3 o'clock
Place: Keys Elementary School

Let's make the world a joyful place!

On Your Own

Look over your invitation and set some lines in boldface or italic. Make any other formatting changes to make the invitation look the way you want it to. Don't you feel happy now?

PART 2

Travel Time

Let's look at my spreadsheet. In column B, I have put the number 6 in each cell, which is the number of hours we want to drive each day. In the cells in column C, I have given the various speeds we may be traveling at.

Let's create a formula in the spreadsheet to multiply the hours times the speed. The answer will appear in column D. Column D will tell us how many miles we can travel in one day at each speed.

1. Click in cell D6.

We will type our multiplication formula, which will also appear in the formula bar at the top of the page. The sign for multiplication is an asterisk (*).

2. Type *=PRODUCT(B6*C6).*
3. Tap **Enter**.

Does cell D6 show 390? Good. That is how many miles we can go if we drive for 6 hours at 65 miles per hour!

	A	B	C	D	E
1				Your name	
2		**My Mileage Calculations: 1,200 miles from Cincinnati to Miami**			
3					
4					
5		Hours	Speed (m.p.h.)	Miles covered	How many days at this speed?
6	What if we drive	6	65	390	
7	What if we drive	6	60		
8	What if we drive	6	55		
9	What if we drive	6	50		
10	What if we drive	6	45		

Bernie's Typing Activities

Open your word processor.
Key the drill lines.

Reinforce: right shift, b, v, comma, x, colon

all letters learned

1. Jr. flakes cup design those woman yield;
2. Jr. flakes cup design those woman yield;

right shift

3. Florida | South Carolina | Arkansas | Colorado
4. Florida | South Carolina | Arkansas | Colorado

b emphasis

5. Bart and Barbara saw a big black baboon.
6. Bart and Barbara saw a big black baboon.

v emphasis

7. Val saved five valves; Vic saved seven.
8. Val saved five valves; Vic saved seven.

comma emphasis

9. Ann, Ben, Ted, and Sam went to the play.
10. Ann, Ben, Ted, and Sam went to the play.

x emphasis

11. Six tax experts voted on the excise tax.
12. Six tax experts voted on the excise tax.

colon emphasis

13. Dear Maria: To: From: Date: Subject:
14. Dear Maria: To: From: Date: Subject:

Project 15

Use a Spreadsheet to Calculate Driving Time

I am excited! My family and I are going on a vacation. We will travel 1,200 miles from Cincinnati, Ohio, all the way to Miami, Florida. I need to figure out how many days it will take us to get there. We think that we can drive six hours a day.

I will use a spreadsheet to figure out how many miles we will drive each day. Will you help me? I am all packed and ready to go!

PART 1

Starting Out

I have already started my spreadsheet. Let's open it now.

1. Open your spreadsheet program.
2. Open the file named *trip*.
3. Choose **Save As** from the **File** menu, and name the file *trip15*.
4. Click on cell **D1**.
5. Type your name in the cell.
6. Tap **Enter**.
7. Save the file again.

Side Trips with Blueberry and Jess

Language Arts

Create Using your computer, write an invitation to a birthday party. Does your party have a theme? Choose a font that fits this theme. Use color, graphics, and layout and design skills to create an eye-catching invitation. Use your thesaurus to find precise and descriptive words. Be sure to check your spelling by using the spelling checker. Save your file as *my invitation5*.

Language Arts

Write Find out more about World Smile Day. Use the Internet or your library to find information. Write an article for your school newspaper about this event. Use Landscape orientation to write your article. Explain the origins and purpose of this day. Write a catchy title and set it in a large font size. Use design and layout skills to design your article. Add clip art.

Project 15

Spreadsheet

Road Trip!

In this project you will:

- Use a spreadsheet to solve problems
- Insert data in a spreadsheet
- Use formulas
- Add borders and shading

Word Power

average

formula

Project 6

Internet

All About E-mail

In this project you will:

- Use e-mail
- Identify the parts of an e-mail message
- Send e-mail
- Receive e-mail
- Reply to e-mail

Word Power

address

e-mail

offline

online

Side Trips with Blueberry and Jess

Health

Record Create a spreadsheet that keeps track of your height over time. You can also keep track of the heights of your friends or your brothers and sisters too. Enter your height over the course of several months (or years—you can call your doctor or ask the school nurse for this information). Enter the data in decimal form, not fractions. For example, type *4* if you are 4 feet tall. Type *4.5* if you are 4 1/2 feet tall. Create a line graph from the spreadsheet that shows how you (and the others) have grown over time.

Music

Track Modify the spreadsheet named *meals14* to show which songs over a four-week period are the most popular. Use the names of songs as your column headings. Then find out which song is rated as number one, number two, and so on each week. Create a line graph from this information.

Send an E-mail Message

Using the Time Machine to travel back in time makes learning about American history exciting. I have learned so much about the Revolutionary War. I want to stay in Boston longer. I have so much to tell Professor Keys. Lucky for me that I brought along my laptop computer! I can use it to send an e-mail message to Professor Keys, telling her what I have learned.

An e-mail message can go from one computer to another computer across the country or across the world in minutes. Let's see if my message can travel through time!

PART 1

The Ins and Outs of E-mail

Did you know that the term e-mail is short for electronic mail? Like regular mail, we use mailboxes to send and receive messages. The difference is that the mailboxes are in an e-mail program on the computer.

Bernie's Typing Activities

Key each drill line twice; key each paragraph once.

Reinforce: 7 & 3

1. The test covers pages 73 to 137 and 177.
2. Only 17 out of 33 seniors took the exam.
3. Reserve May 13 and 17 and June 7 and 13.
4. Study Chapters 3, 7, 13, 14, 17, and 19.
5. Zane said 37.13 plus 73.37 equals 110.5.

Who Am I?

I became the President of the United States in 1933. When I was President, there were two major events that took place.

The first event was the Great Depression. The second event was World War II. I was the only President to be elected to four terms in office. Who am I?

Here is what my e-mail program looks like. Your e-mail program may look a little different.

Create Mail or **New** button: Click on this button to type a new e-mail message.

Inbox: Mail you receive comes into the Inbox.

Outbox: Mail you send goes into the Outbox.

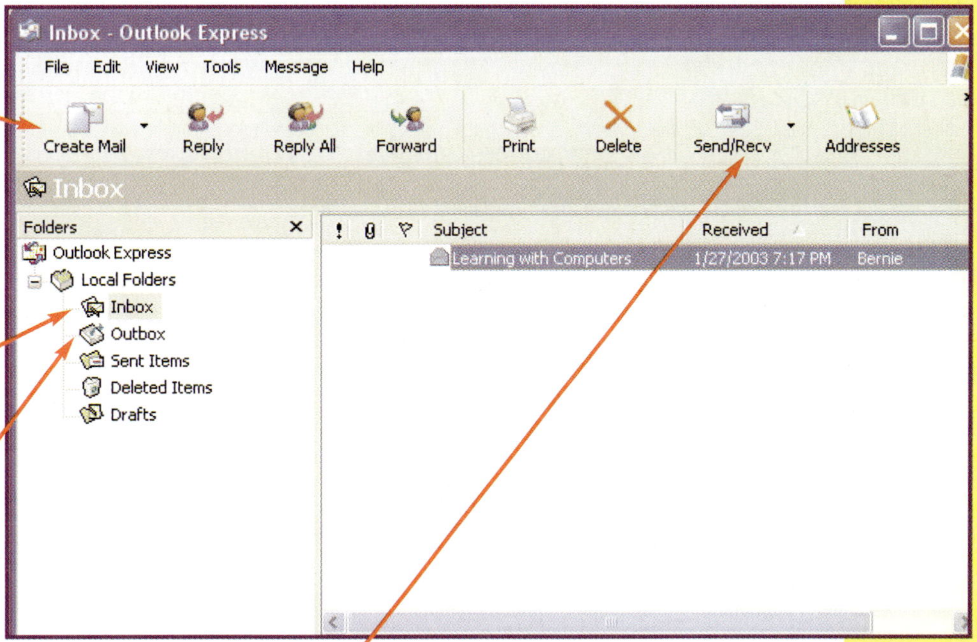

Send & Receive button: Click on this button to get your e-mail.

1. Open your e-mail software program.
2. Find the parts shown above on your e-mail screen.
3. Click on the **Create Mail** or **New** button to create a new e-mail message.

Quick Check

Good job! Now your spreadsheet is ready. I am getting hungry. Is it time for lunch?

	A	B	C	D	E
1	Your name				
2					
3		Number of Meals Students Ate			
4					
5		Hamburger	Tofu Burger	Macaroni and Cheese	Salad Plate
6	Week 1	11	5	10	7
7	Week 2	9	8	8	9
8	Week 3	8	10	7	12
9	Week 4	6	12	6	13
10	Totals	34	35	31	41

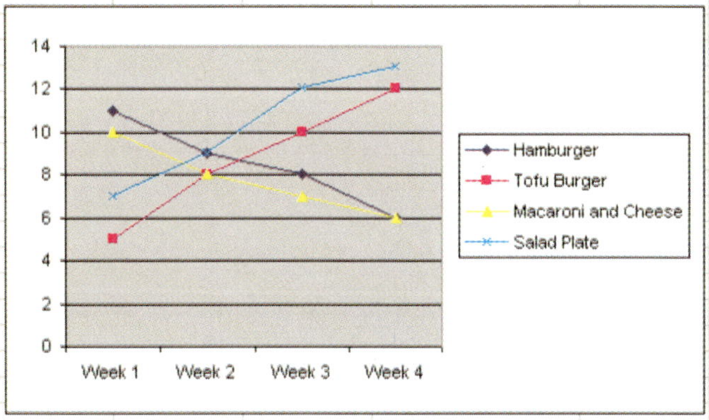

On Your Own

Add another column to the spreadsheet. Think of another meal that could be served. Add the name of the meal to cell F5. Then add data in column F. Use the Autosum button to find the total. Add clip art. Create a new line graph. Save your revised spreadsheet as my meals14.

Your new e-mail message screen may look like this.

Send button: Click on this button to send an e-mail.

To field: Type the e-mail address of the person you are writing to here.

Subject field: Type what the message is about here.

Message area: Type your message here.

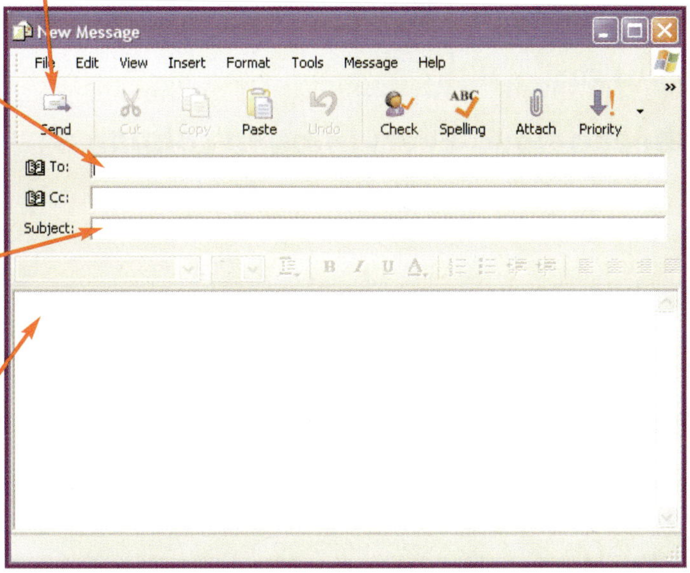

*The **Cc** field is used to send a copy of an e-mail to another person.*

PART 2

Type a Message

When you write a letter, you write the letter first and then you write the address on the envelope. When you send an e-mail, you start with the address and then you type the message. We are going to send an e-mail to Professor Keys. Her e-mail address is profkeys@swlearning.com.

Centering the numbers and column headings can make a spreadsheet look better. You can center one cell at a time, or you can highlight a column or row or the whole table and center the entire highlighted area. Try it!

1. Select column B.
2. Click the **Center** button.

Look at the spreadsheet below. Everything in column B is centered.

	A	B	C	D	E
1	Your name				
2					
3					
4					
5		Hamburger	Tofu Burger	Macaroni and Cheese	Salad Plate
6	Week 1	11	5	10	7
7	Week 2	9	8	8	9
8	Week 3	8	10	7	12
9	Week 4	6	12	6	13
10	Totals	34	35	31	41

3. Select the columns C, D, and E and center the data.

Now let's make the column headings bold.

4. Select the column headings in B5 to E5.
5. Click on the **Bold** button.
6. Place your cursor in cell B3 and type the title ***Number of Meals Students Ate***.
7. Change the font, font size, and color of the title. The choice is yours!
8. Save your work.

If you make the column headings bold, you may need to widen the columns.

***An e-mail address always has the @ symbol, pronounced "at." The period is always called a dot. So you would say Professor Keys' address as* profkeys at s w learning dot com.**

An e-mail address has three parts:

profkeys = mailbox (some people use their own name, nickname, or other name)

swlearning = the domain, usually the name of the Internet provider

.com = the zone tells what kind of site you are visiting (some other zones are: .net, .edu, .org)

I want to tell Professor Keys some reasons why Americans wanted to declare their independence from England. Let's do it together!

1. Click on **New** to open a new message window.
2. Click in the **To** field.
3. Type Professor Keys' e-mail address, *profkeys@swlearning.com*.
4. Tap the **Tab** key or use your mouse to move your cursor to the **Subject** field.
5. Type *Taxes* in the **Subject** field.
6. Move to the message area.

PART 5

Adding Eye Appeal

You can make your spreadsheet easier to read. You learned in Project 13 how to add borders and shading to a spreadsheet. Let's add shading to the row and column headings. Adding a title is always a good idea!

Excel

1. Select cells A6 to A10.
2. Choose **Cells** from the **Format** menu.
3. Click on the **Patterns** tab.
4. Select a color.
5. Click **OK**.
6. Save your work.

AppleWorks

1. Select cells A6 to A10.
2. Choose **Show Tools** from the **Window** menu.
3. Click on the **Color palette** button.
4. Select a color.
5. Save your work.

Now choose a shading color for the column headings!

Excel

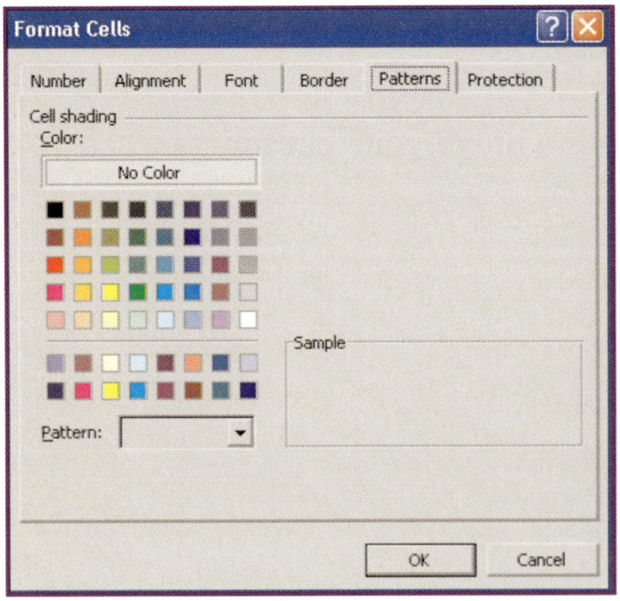

AppleWorks

7 Type the message shown below.

Dear Professor Keys,

The colonists were angry about the unfair taxes. They felt that they had no representatives in the English Parliament to present their side. The Patriots called this "taxation without representation."

Your friend,
Bernie Mouse

If your e-mail program has a spelling checker, check your e-mail. If not, proofread it carefully!

Quick Check

You are doing a great job! Your e-mail message should look like this. If not, try the steps again.

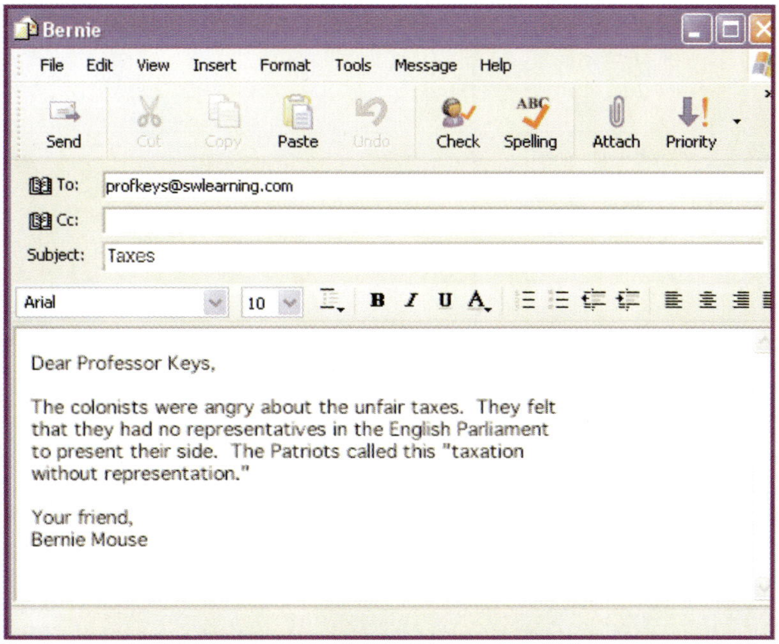

Quick Check

Your spreadsheet should look like this now. Does your line graph match the information in your chart? The graph shows that the tofu burger has become more popular each week. Macaroni and cheese has grown less popular.

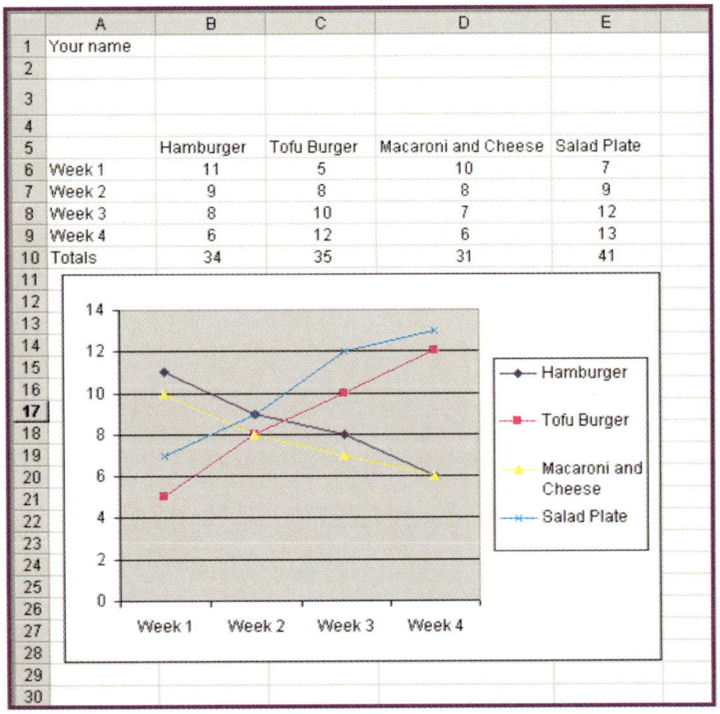

	A	B	C	D	E
1	Your name				
2					
3					
4					
5		Hamburger	Tofu Burger	Macaroni and Cheese	Salad Plate
6	Week 1	11	5	10	7
7	Week 2	9	8	8	9
8	Week 3	8	10	7	12
9	Week 4	6	12	6	13
10	Totals	34	35	31	41

If you are using ***Excel*** *and your chart does not look like this, click on the* ***Next*** *button in the* ***Chart Wizard****. Then select* ***Columns*** *in the* ***Series in*** *section.*

Jake's Ergonomics Tip

Sometimes you can hurt the muscles in your hand or wrist by gripping the mouse too tightly. Take a break and open and close your hand a few times.

PART 3

It Is in the Mail!

To send and receive e-mail, you have to be connected to the Internet. However, you can write your e-mails and read messages that you have received when you are not connected. This is called working offline. To send your message, you have to be online, or connected to the Internet. Let's get connected now! Ask your teacher when you are online.

1. Click on the **Send** button to send your e-mail to Professor Keys.

Now send an e-mail to a classmate.

2. Click on the **Create Mail** or **New** button to create a new e-mail message.
3. Type your classmate's e-mail address in the **To** field.
4. Type *Hello* in the **Subject** field.
5. Type a message.

   Hi, [Your Classmate's Name]
   I want to receive a reply to this e-mail.

6. Click on the **Send** button.

You should receive a reply in a few minutes. While you are waiting, look back at your file named causes4. Be prepared for Professor Keys to ask you some questions!

You can use smileys or emoticons in your e-mails to show expression. Here are a few that I use. Do you know more?

[ ]	Hug
B)	Cool smiley sunglasses
:O	Yelling
;)	Winking smiley face
:(	Frowney
:<	Sad
= o	Surprised

PART 4

Create a Line Graph

Now that I have all the data, how can I figure out which meals are the most popular? A line graph would really help me. A line graph shows how data changes over time. Here, it will show how popular a meal was over the course of four weeks.

You created a column or bar chart in Project 13. Do you remember? You follow many of the same steps to create a line graph.

1. Select rows 5 through 9.
2. Click on the **Chart** button on the toolbar.
3. Choose **Line** from the graph types.
4. Click the picture of the type of line graph that you would like to use.
5. Click on **Finish** or **OK**.
6. Resize the line graph so that it looks like the one shown on the next page.
7. Save your work.

Click on **Line** graph.

Excel

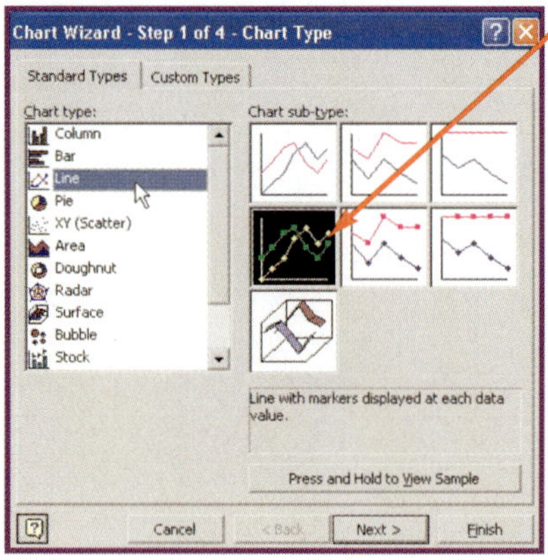

AppleWorks

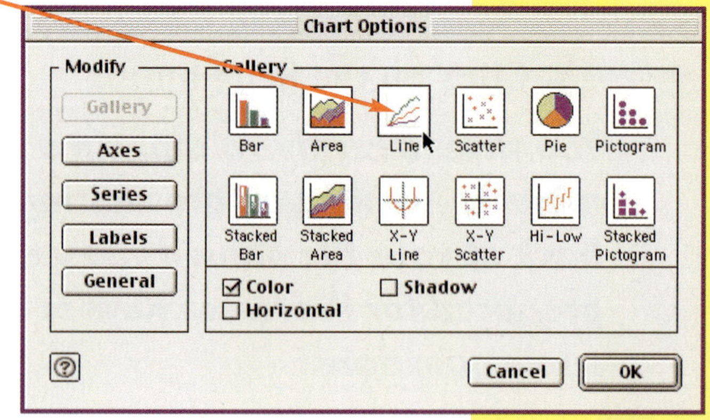

PART 4

Check Your Inbox

Now it is time to check your e-mail! You should expect to find two messages in your Inbox. One will be from Professor Keys. The other one will be from a classmate.

Inbox

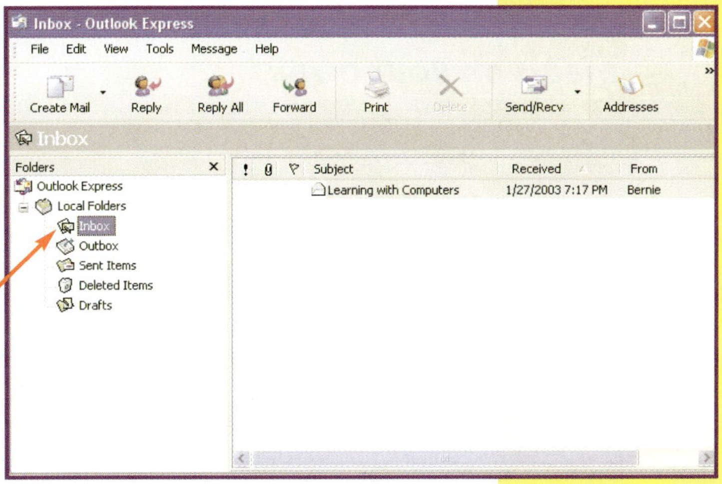

1. Click on the **Send & Receive** button.
2. Find the **Inbox** for your e-mail program.

New messages should be in bold.

3. Click once on the message that your classmate sent you.

It will open up.

4. Read the message.

Jake's Ergonomics Tip

Make sure your monitor is at eye level so that you are not straining your neck muscles. Some monitors can be tilted or placed on a stand. You may be able to adjust your chair to raise or lower it.

3. Click on cell C6 and select the range of cells C6 to C10.
4. Click on the **Autosum** button.

This is easy! You can add the totals for the next three meals on your own.

Quick Check

Nice work! Do your totals match the totals in the spreadsheet below?

	A	B	C	D	E	F
1	Your name					
2						
3						
4						
5		Hamburger	Tofu Burger	Macaroni and Cheese	Fish Sticks	Salad Plate
6	Week 1	11	5	10	3	7
7	Week 2	9	8	8	2	9
8	Week 3	8	10	7	1	12
9	Week 4	6	12	6	1	13
10	Totals	34	35	31	7	41
11						

5. Save your work.

It is very clear that fish sticks are not too popular. We can delete this column from our spreadsheet now.

6. Click on the letter E at the top of the column.

The entire column should be selected.

Excel

7. Choose **Delete** from the **Edit** menu.
8. Save your work.

AppleWorks

7. Choose **Delete Cells** from the **Format** menu.
8. Save your work.

Column E should now say* Salad Plate. *Does it? You are a real pro!

Now try sending a reply to that message.

5 Click on the **Reply** button.

You should have a new message window.
The message is already addressed to your classmate, with a return address from you.

Reply button

6 Type this message to your classmate.

I know how to create a new e-mail message, send it, receive it, and even reply to it!

7 Add an emoticon, or smiley, to your message.

8 Click on the **Send** button.

Using e-mail is so easy!

*You can also print e-mails that you send or receive. Use the **Print** button on the toolbar, or choose **Print** from the **File** menu.*

On Your Own

When you receive a message from Professor Keys, use the Reply button to thank her for sending you an e-mail. Tell her what you know about the Boston Tea Party.

Quick Check

Your spreadsheet should look like this.

	A	B	C	D	E	F
1	Your name					
2						
3						
4						
5		Hamburger	Tofu Burger	Macaroni and Cheese	Fish Sticks	Salad Plate
6	Week 1	11	5	10	3	7
7	Week 2	9	8	8	2	9
8	Week 3	8	10	7	1	12
9	Week 4	6	12	6	1	13
10	Totals					
11						

PART 3

The Most Popular Meals

We have put in all our numbers, but now we need to find the totals. We can use the Autosum button to add the numbers for us.

1. Click on cell B6 and select the range of cells B6 to B10.
2. Click on the **Autosum** button on the toolbar. Σ

Cell B10 should have the number 34 now. That is the total number of students who ate hamburgers over the course of four weeks. Now let's add the numbers in column C.

Bernie's Typing Activities

Open your word processor. Key the drill lines.

Review

all letters learned

1 just know deal fish box cymbal gap rove;
2 just know deal fish box cymbal gap rove;

double letters

3 Jill took her old college books to sell.
4 Jill took her old college books to sell.

shift keys

5 I have lived in San Diego and St. Louis.
6 I have lived in San Diego and St. Louis.

b/y (long reaches)

7 gym buy young by knob yarn barely doubts
8 gym buy young by knob yarn barely doubts

one-hand words

9 state look area milk draft only tax were
10 state look area milk draft only tax were

balanced-hand sentences

11 Jane paid the men for the work they did.
12 Jane paid the men for the work they did.

13 Eight of the girls may go to the social.
14 Eight of the girls may go to the social.

4. Ten students ate macaroni and cheese in Week 1. Click on cell D6 and type *10*.
5. Three students ate fish sticks in Week 1. Click on cell E6 and type *3*.
6. Seven students ate the salad plate in Week 1. Click on cell F6 and type *7*.
7. Save your work.

	A	B	C	D	E	F
1	Your name					
2						
3						
4						
5		Hamburger	Tofu Burger	Macaroni and Cheese	Fish Sticks	Salad Plate
6	Week 1	11	5	10	3	7
7	Week 2					
8	Week 3					
9	Week 4					
10	Totals					
11						
12						

Now use the data on my notepad to fill in the rest of the columns. Start with Week 2 and work your way across the columns. Remember to save your work after you have entered all the data!

	Hamburger	Tofu Burger	Macaroni and Cheese	Fish Sticks	Salad Plate
Week 1	11	5	10	3	7
Week 2	9	8	8	2	9
Week 3	8	10	7	1	12
Week 4	6	12	6	1	13

Side Trips with Blueberry and Jess

Social Studies

Write Read your file named *causes4* that you created in Project 4. Look up the meaning of the words *veto*, *regulated*, and *taxation*. Write these words and their definitions as an e-mail message. Be sure to check your spelling. Find the spelling checker on your e-mail program. Then send your e-mail to your teacher.

Language Arts

Write *Etiquette* means "rules of good behavior." Here are some rules of good behavior, or netiquette, for using e-mail. Type this list into an e-mail message. Send the message to someone you know, or just print a copy of the message. Always follow these rules when you use e-mail!

Bernie's E-mail Netiquette Rules

- Only send e-mail to people with the permission of your parents or teacher.
- Do not use all capital letters in e-mail messages. People call this shouting. It is not a polite thing to do.
- Do not send an e-mail that is impolite or will hurt someone's feelings.
- Be careful what you type in an e-mail. People will not know if you are joking. You might want to use a smiley, such as :).
- Respect other people's privacy. Do not read other people's e-mails.
- Do not share your password with anyone else. Passwords are private and are not safe to share with others.

Quick Check

Does your spreadsheet look like this?
If not, make any changes now.

	A	B	C	D	E	F
1	Your name					
2						
3						
4						
5		Hamburger	Tofu Burger	Macaroni and Cheese	Fish Sticks	Salad Plate
6	Week 1					
7	Week 2					
8	Week 3					
9	Week 4					
10	Totals					
11						
12						

PART 2

Lunchtime Choices

Now we are ready to start entering our data. I have a list of which meals students chose. Let's start entering the data for Week 1.

1. Move to cell B6.
2. Eleven students ate hamburgers in Week 1. Type *11* in cell B6.
3. Five students ate tofu burgers in Week 1. Click on cell C6 and type *5*.

Project
7

Internet and Word Processing

Searching the Internet

In this project you will:

- Use the Internet
- Enter a URL
- Use toolbar buttons to navigate the Internet
- Set an Internet bookmark
- Use a search engine

Word Power

Address bar

bookmark

graphic

home page

hyperlink

search engine

URL

Web browser

Web page

Web site

Use the name box in the upper left corner to be sure you are in the right cell.

7. Tap the **Tab** key or use the arrow keys to move to cell B5.
8. Type ***Hamburger*** in cell B5.

Name or Address box

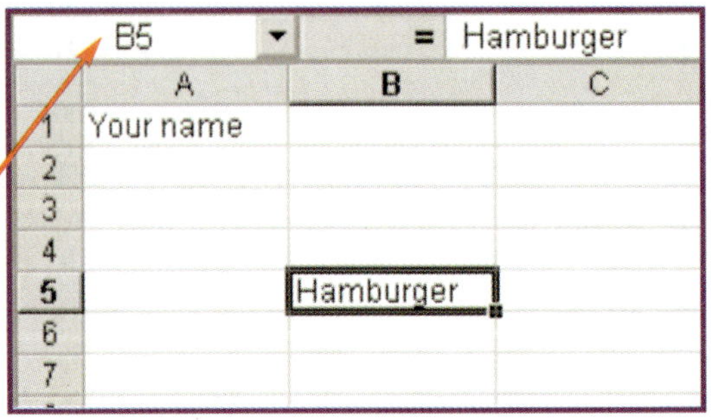

9. Tap the **Tab** key to move to cell C5.
10. Type ***Tofu Burger***.
11. Tap the **Tab** key to move to cell D5.
12. Type ***Macaroni and Cheese***.

You will need to make the column wider to fit these words.

13. Place your pointer at the very top line between columns D and E and drag the column to the right.
14. Move to cell E5.
15. Type ***Fish Sticks***.
16. Move to cell F5.
17. Type ***Salad Plate***.

Now we are ready to add the row headings.

18. Move to cell A6. Type ***Week 1***.
19. Tap **Enter** or **Return** to bring you to cell A7.
20. Type ***Week 2***.
21. Move to cell A8. Type ***Week 3***.
22. Move to cell A9. Type ***Week 4***.
23. Move to cell A10. Type ***Totals***.
24. Save your work.

Project 7

Search for Information on the Internet

Welcome to Boston! The year is 1773, and I have used a Time Machine to travel back in time. I saw a major event called the Boston Tea Party. Patriots dressed as Mohawk Indians threw tea into Boston Harbor to protest a tax on tea. I have written a newspaper article about this event. I think that Samuel Adams was the leader. Will you help me search on the Internet to find out if I am right? We will also find a picture to paste into the article. Let's start our search!

PART 1

What a Story!

Before we go to the Internet, let's read my article.

1. Open the file named *teaparty*.
2. Choose **Save As** from the **File** menu.
3. Name the file *teaparty7*.

Boston Goes Overboard When It Comes to Tea!

Boston, December 17, 1773 Last evening bands of local "Indians" made a big splash to prove that the boycott of tea in Boston was not ending. Witnesses say that three groups of men boarded the three East India Company ships waiting in the harbor to unload their cargo of tea. Each group numbered around 50 men. The men appeared to be dressed as Mohawk Indians. On each ship, they broke open the tea chests and heaved them into the water as the growing crowd onshore cheered.

The identity of the individuals involved is a closely guarded secret because the local citizens want to protect their fellow Patriots. The Boston Tea Party proved that the people fully support the Patriot raiders!

Project 14

Create a Spreadsheet to Track Meals

My school is going to change the lunch menu. The cafeteria manager wants to figure out which meals are the most popular. The most popular choices will stay on the menu and the least popular meals will not be served again. A spreadsheet will help us keep track of how many students chose each meal. Would you like to help me create this spreadsheet? Let's do it together!

PART 1

What's the Plan?

Let's open our spreadsheet program and get to work.

1. Open your spreadsheet program.
2. Click on cell A1.
3. Type your name.
4. Choose **Save** from the **File** menu.
5. In the **File name** box, type ***meals14***.
6. Click on **Save**.

Now let's set up the spreadsheet with column headings and row headings. We will start with the column headings.

PART 2

Find the Best Internet Sites

It's time to get on the Internet to search for the leader of the Boston Tea Party. We will use a Web browser software program to connect to your home page. This page appears every time you connect to the Internet. From your home page, you will need an address, called a URL, to get to a Web site. To get to a Web site successfully, you need to type all the characters in the URL.

Be smart and check out many different resources to make sure your information is correct.

1. Click on your Internet icon to connect to the Internet.
2. Find the Address bar at the top of the screen of the home page.

Type the URL in the **Address** bar.

Go button

3. In the Address bar, type the URL *pbskids.org/libertyskids/*.
4. Click on the **Go** button or tap **Enter**.

All right! You have successfully gone to a Web site. You should see a page that looks like this.

Project 14

Spreadsheet

What's for Lunch?

In this project you will:

- Create a spreadsheet
- Use a spreadsheet to solve problems
- Delete a column
- Insert a line graph
- Add shading
- Center text
- Format text

Word Power

Autosum

line graph

range

***Hyperlinks**, or links, connect one **Web page** to another. They can be words or icons or both. The hand cursor indicates a link. If you click on the icon or words, you will go to another page.*

Remember, we are searching for information about the Boston Tea Party and Samuel Adams. We need to navigate the Web site to find the information we need.

5. Click on *Liberty Archive.*
6. You are at a new page. On this page, click on *WHERE* to find information on famous places and events.
7. You are at a new page. On this page, click on *Boston, Massachusetts*.
8. You are at a new page. On this page, click on *Samuel Adams*.

Are you at this page? Was Samuel Adams a leader in the Boston Tea Party?

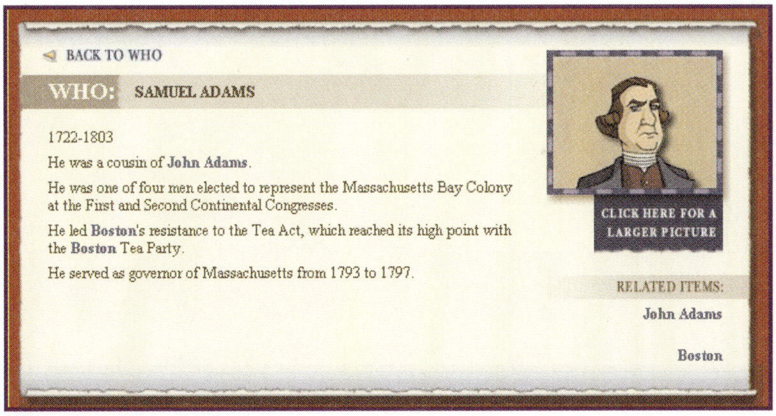

Let's retrace our steps. Let's go back one page at a time until we reach the home page of the Liberty's Kids Web site. We do this by using the Back button on the toolbar.

Side Trips with Blueberry and Jess

Math

Create Design a spreadsheet to track your grades and calculate the average grade for each subject. The spreadsheet will then automatically figure out your grade average. Enter the score you received on each test. To make your spreadsheet easier to read, add borders and shading and make other format changes. Then use the spreadsheet to show how just one bad grade can bring your grade average down or one really good grade can bring your average up. Revise your spreadsheet with your current grades and create a chart. Continue to enter your grades each week. Your spreadsheet should look like this.

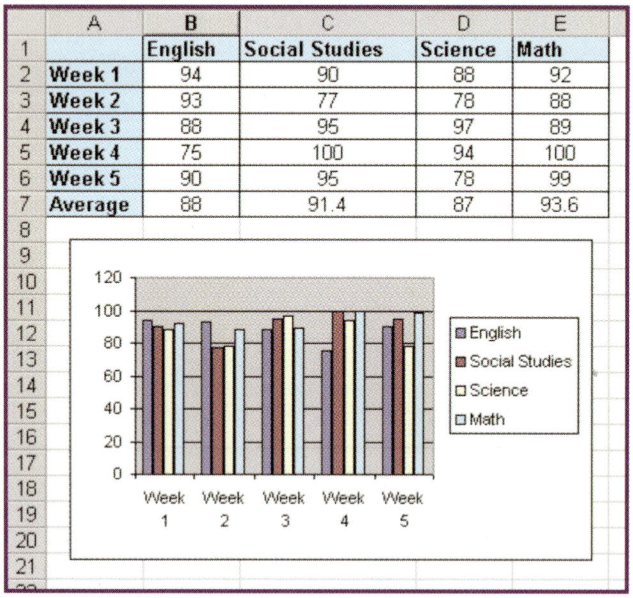

	A	B	C	D	E
1		English	Social Studies	Science	Math
2	Week 1	94	90	88	92
3	Week 2	93	77	78	88
4	Week 3	88	95	97	89
5	Week 4	75	100	94	100
6	Week 5	90	95	78	99
7	Average	88	91.4	87	93.6

9 Click on the **Back** button on the toolbar to go back to the page where we found the link for Boston, Massachusetts.

10 Click on the **Back** button to reach the **WHERE** page.

11 Click on the **Back** button to reach the page for the Liberty Archive.

12 Click on the **Back** button to reach the home page.

Super! Now if you want to go to the page about Samuel Adams, you should use the Forward button.

PART 3

Set a Bookmark

The Liberty's Kids Web site is a good one! You will want to return to it again. You can set a bookmark to go right to this site without typing in the URL. Look at the toolbar at the top of your browser. Your browser has a great tool called Favorites or Bookmarks. When you are on the Liberty's Kids Web site, add a bookmark to save the URL. Let's set a bookmark for Liberty's Kids.

1 Click on the **Favorites** menu option.

2 Choose **Add . . .**

3 Click on the **OK** button.

The name for the new bookmark is shown here.

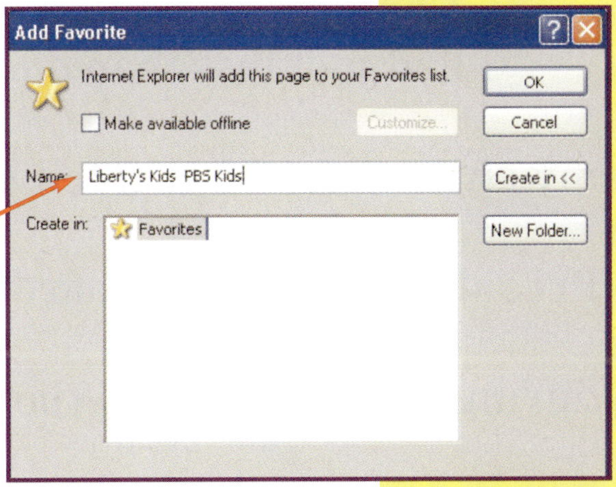

Excellent! Let's try it out!

Bernie's Typing Activities

Key each drill line twice; key each paragraph once.

Reinforce: 0 & 5

1. Our 2003 profit was up by 50.05 percent.
2. For 2003 my tax was 15.5 percent higher.
3. The numbers were 505A, 505A1, and 505A5.
4. We moved from 1500 Zeitz to 501 Fairfax.
5. By adding 5 plus 50 to 500, you get 555.

Who Am I?

I was born in a log cabin in Kentucky in 1890. I became quite skilled at using an axe to make fence rails. When I ran for President, I became known as the Rail Splitter.

I had just less than one year of formal education my entire life. I educated myself; I loved to read. As President, I fought hard to preserve the Union during the Civil War. Who am I?

4. Use the **Back** button to return to your browser's home page.
5. Click on the **Favorites** menu.
6. Choose the Liberty's Kids bookmark.

Wow! You did it! You should be back at the Liberty's Kids Web site. If you are not, do the steps again.

PART 4

The Search Engine That Could

***How do you find information if you do not have a Web site address? This question is easy to answer. We can use a search engine to help us find information on the Internet. A search engine is a software program that searches all Web sites using the words you enter. Let's start by doing a simple search using the words* Boston Tea Party.**

1. Type *google.com* in the **Address** bar, then click on the **Go** button or tap **Enter**.
2. Type *Boston Tea Party* in the **Search** box.
3. Click on the **Google Search** button.

Jake's Ergonomics Tip

When you sit at the computer, keep your feet flat on the floor. This keeps your blood flowing better so that your heart doesn't have to work as hard.

PART 7

Chart It!

One other interesting thing you can do is to include a chart in your spreadsheet. You can turn the data in your spreadsheet into a chart that is easy to read. To make a chart, follow these steps.

1. Select cells A4 to D10.
2. Click on the **Chart** button on the toolbar. 
3. In the box, click on the **Column** or **Bar** chart.
4. Click on **Finish** or **OK**.
5. Save your work.

Your chart will appear on your spreadsheet. The bars in the chart should be labeled with the days of the week. The legend shows which bars stand for Jess, Bernie, and Jake.

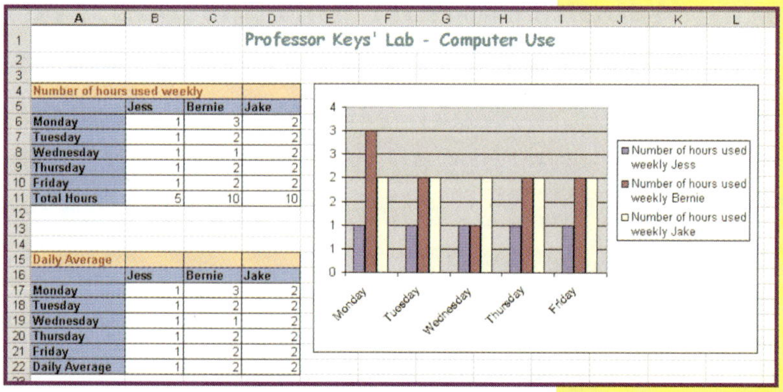

Professor Keys' Lab - Computer Use

Number of hours used weekly	Jess	Bernie	Jake
Monday	1	3	2
Tuesday	1	2	2
Wednesday	1	1	2
Thursday	1	2	2
Friday	1	2	2
Total Hours	5	10	10

Daily Average	Jess	Bernie	Jake
Monday	1	3	2
Tuesday	1	2	2
Wednesday	1	1	2
Thursday	1	2	2
Friday	1	2	2
Daily Average	1	2	2

Thanks for all your hard work. Using a spreadsheet is a good way to solve math problems!

On Your Own

Modify the spreadsheet to keep track of how many hours a day you and other members of your family use a computer.

Look at all the Web sites that were found! To go to one of the sites, you click on the name. Before you start clicking, however, check the name of the person or organization that created this site. The information may not always be accurate! The two sites listed below would be good choices. One is by PBS, or Public Television. The other is a museum Web site.

Boston Tea Party Ship and Museum
... **Boston Tea Party** Ship sm and Museum Congress Street Bridge - **Boston**, Massachusetts 02210 Telephone: (617) 338-1773 Fax: (617) 338 ...
www.bostonteapartyship.com/History.htm - 15k - Cached - Similar pages
[More results from www.bostonteapartyship.com]

Boston Tea Party
THE **BOSTON TEA PARTY**. The **Boston Tea Party** was one of the most effective pieces of political theater ever staged. John Adams, no ...
Description: Video and audio clips by scholar Pauline Maier for PBS.
Category: Regional > North America > ... > Boston Tea Party
www.pbs.org/ktca/liberty/chronicle/ bostonteaparty-edenton.html - 13k - Feb 4, 2003 - Cached - Similar pages

The site is by PBS.

4. Click on the PBS Web site named ***Boston Tea Party***.

A screen like this one should appear.

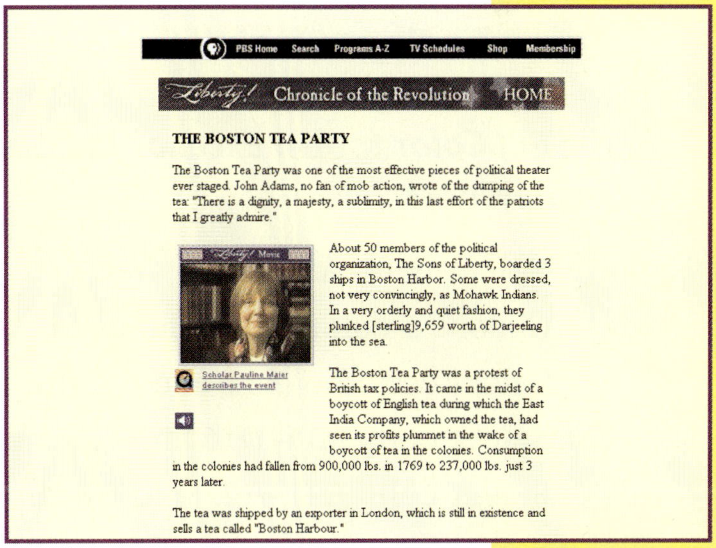

PBS Home Search Programs A-Z TV Schedules Shop Membership
Liberty! Chronicle of the Revolution HOME

THE BOSTON TEA PARTY

The Boston Tea Party was one of the most effective pieces of political theater ever staged. John Adams, no fan of mob action, wrote of the dumping of the tea: "There is a dignity, a majesty, a sublimity, in this last effort of the patriots that I greatly admire."

About 50 members of the political organization, The Sons of Liberty, boarded 3 ships in Boston Harbor. Some were dressed, not very convincingly, as Mohawk Indians. In a very orderly and quiet fashion, they plunked [sterling]9,659 worth of Darjeeling into the sea.

Scholar Pauline Maier describes the event

The Boston Tea Party was a protest of British tax policies. It came in the midst of a boycott of English tea during which the East India Company, which owned the tea, had seen its profits plummet in the wake of a boycott of tea in the colonies. Consumption in the colonies had fallen from 900,000 lbs. in 1769 to 237,000 lbs. just 3 years later.

The tea was shipped by an exporter in London, which is still in existence and sells a tea called "Boston Harbour."

Put your cursor on the picture. You will see a moving picture and hear the author talk! This Web site is a good one! Set a bookmark to this page.

5. Click on the **Favorites** button.
6. Choose **Add . . .**

Now let's format the days of the week and the three names in both tables to make them stand out.

7. Select column A.
8. Click on the **Bold** button on the toolbar.
9. Select row 5 and click on the **Bold** button.
10. Select row 16 and click on the **Bold** button.

When you make the words bold, you may need to adjust the column width.

	A	B	C	D
1				Professor Keys' Lab - Computer Use
2				
3				
4	Number of hours used weekly			
5		Jess	Bernie	Jake
6	Monday	1	3	2
7	Tuesday	1	2	2
8	Wednesday	1	1	2
9	Thursday	1	2	2
10	Friday	1	2	2
11	Total Hours	5	10	10
12				
13				
14				
15	Daily Average			
16		Jess	Bernie	Jake
17	Monday	1	3	2
18	Tuesday	1	2	2
19	Wednesday	1	1	2
20	Thursday	1	2	2
21	Friday	1	2	2
22	Daily Average	1	2	2

Apply shading to the column headings and row headings to make the spreadsheet easier to read. It's easy. Just use the Fill Color tool in Excel or the Color palette button in AppleWorks.

11. Select cells A5–D5.
12. Choose a color to fill the cells.
13. Select cells A6–A11 and fill the cells with color.
14. Select cells A16–D16 and fill the cells with color.
15. Select cells A17–A22 and fill the cells with color.
16. Save your work.

Advanced Searches

***When we used the search engine, we entered the words* Boston Tea Party. *We can narrow our search by using more specific words. We can type* Boston Tea Party AND Samuel Adams. *The word* AND *tells the search engine that we are looking for material with information on* both, *and nothing less will do. Try it! Your search will give you Web sites that are different from the ones you found when you just typed* Boston Tea Party.**

1. Navigate back to *google.com*.
2. Type the words *Boston Tea Party AND Samuel Adams* in the **Search** box.
3. Click on the **Google Search** button or tap **Enter**.

You should see a page similar to this one.

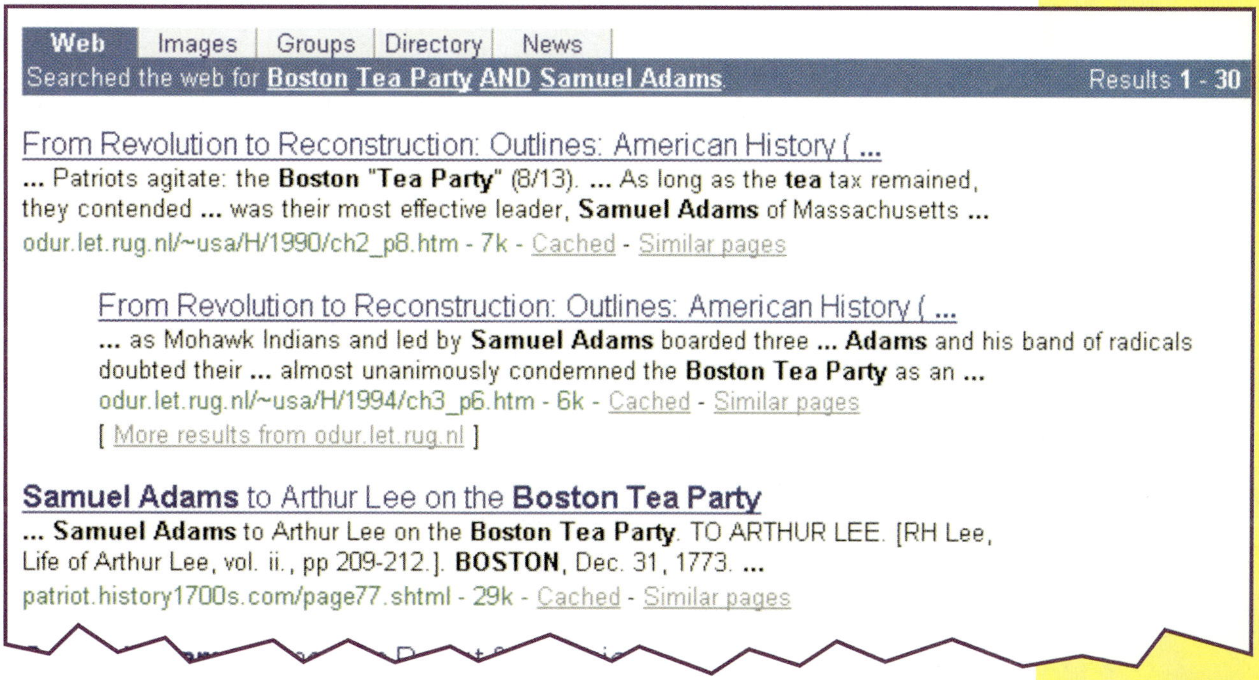

PART 6

Make It Beautiful

You have a lot of information in your spreadsheet now. You can use boldface, borders, and shading to make the spreadsheet easier to read. You can also change the sizes of the letters and numbers in the cells.

To add borders around the cells, follow these steps.

1. Select cells A4–D11.

Excel

2. Click on the drop-down arrow on the **Borders** button on the toolbar.

3. Select the **All Border** option.

AppleWorks

2. Click on the **Border** buttons called **Outline Border**, **Left Border**, **Top Border**, **Right Border**, and **Bottom Border**.

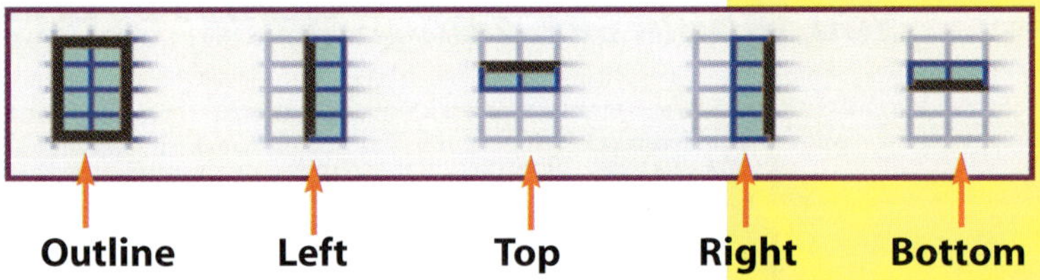

Use the same steps to add a border around the Daily Average table.

1. Select cells A15–D22.
2. Add a border.
3. Save the file.

Your spreadsheet should look like this now.

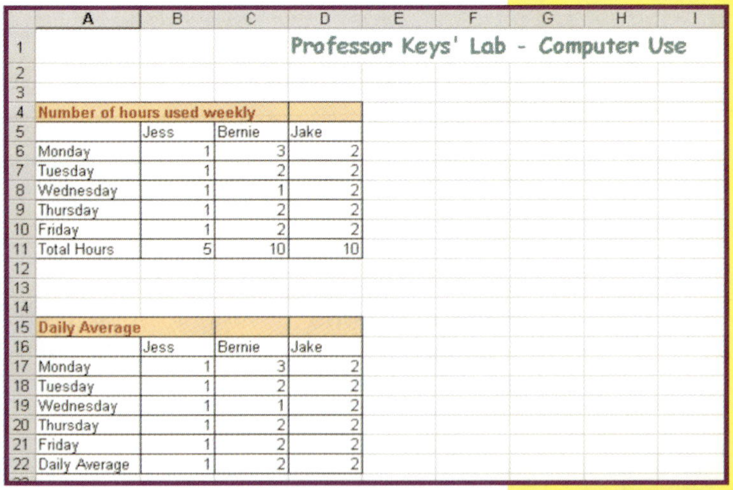

Professor Keys' Lab - Computer Use

Number of hours used weekly			
	Jess	Bernie	Jake
Monday	1	3	2
Tuesday	1	2	2
Wednesday	1	1	2
Thursday	1	2	2
Friday	1	2	2
Total Hours	5	10	10

Daily Average			
	Jess	Bernie	Jake
Monday	1	3	2
Tuesday	1	2	2
Wednesday	1	1	2
Thursday	1	2	2
Friday	1	2	2
Daily Average	1	2	2

PART 6

Back at the Word Processor

Did you find out who was responsible for the Boston Tea Party? Good work! Our research on the Internet has paid off! Now you can add the important information to my report that Samuel Adams was the leader of the Boston Tea Party. Keep your Web browser software program open when you open the file in your word processing program. You will use both programs.

1. Open the file *teaparty7*.
2. Place your cursor just after the next-to-the-last sentence, "The identity of the individuals involved is a closely guarded secret because the local citizens want to protect their fellow Patriots."
3. Type a sentence about what you discovered through your research.
4. Save the file.

Now add a picture, or graphic, at the bottom of the article. Return to the Web sites you bookmarked. Find a graphic you like. Maybe you will choose a picture of Samuel Adams. Or you could choose a picture of a Boston Tea Party ship.

5. Minimize the size of the Web site screen so that you can see your file.
6. Right-click on the graphic you want to use.
7. Choose **Copy** from the **Edit** menu.
8. Use the taskbar to go back to your file *teaparty7*.

If you are using AppleWorks, place your cursor at the end of your file. Click and drag the picture to insert it at the end of your file.

Now calculate the daily average for Bernie and Jake.

Excel

1. Click on cell C22.
2. Choose **Function** from the **Insert** menu.
3. Click on **AVERAGE**.
4. Click on **OK** and click on **OK** again.
5. Click on cell D22.
6. Choose **Function** from the **Insert** menu.
7. Click on **AVERAGE**.
8. Click on **OK** and click on **OK** again.
9. Save the file.

AppleWorks

1. Select cells C17:C22.
2. Choose **Auto Average** from the **Calculate** menu.
3. Select cells D17:D22.
4. Choose **Auto Average** from the **Calculate** menu.
5. Save the file.

Quick Check

Super! Your spreadsheet should look like this now. Check row 22. If your numbers do not match the numbers in the spreadsheet shown, check your work again.

	A	B	C	D
1				Professor Keys' Lab - Computer Use
2				
3				
4	Number of hours used weekly			
5		Jess	Bernie	Jake
6	Monday	1	3	2
7	Tuesday	1	2	2
8	Wednesday	1	1	2
9	Thursday	1	2	2
10	Friday	1	2	2
11	Total Hours	5	10	10
12				
13				
14				
15	Daily Average			
16		Jess	Bernie	Jake
17	Monday	1	3	2
18	Tuesday	1	2	2
19	Wednesday	1	1	2
20	Thursday	1	2	2
21	Friday	1	2	2
22	Daily Average	1	2	2

9. Place your cursor at the end of your file.
10. Click on the **Paste** button to insert the graphic into the file.
11. Resize the graphic to make it fit.
12. Save the file.

Great work! Your research skills are improving every day!

On Your Own

Search the Internet for information on Paul Revere. Was he involved in the Boston Tea Party? Find out if he was one of the raiding Mohawks. Add a paragraph about Paul Revere to the teaparty7 file.

Great job! Now we have a copy of our table!

5. Click on cell A15.
6. Delete the text and type *Daily Average.*
7. Click on row 22.
8. Delete the text and type *Daily Average* in cell A22.

Now let's calculate the daily average.

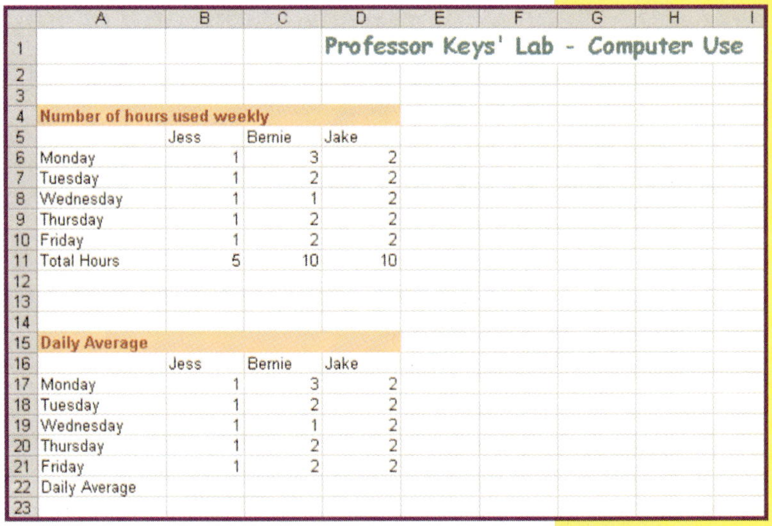

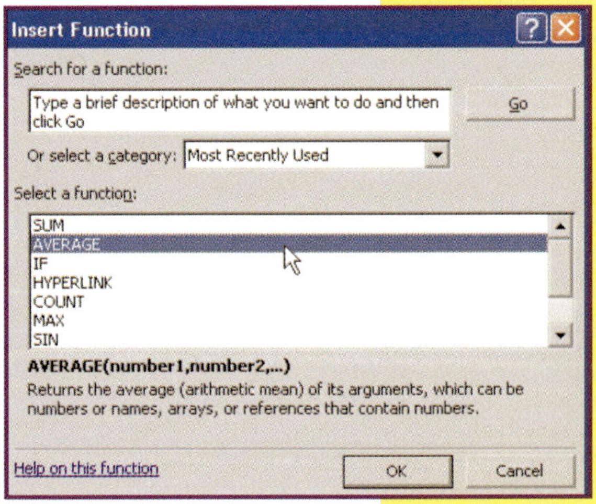

Excel

9. Click on cell B22.
10. Choose **Function** from the **Insert** menu.
11. Click on **AVERAGE**.
12. Click on **OK**.
13. A dialog box with B17:B21 appears in the **Number 1** box. Click on **OK**.

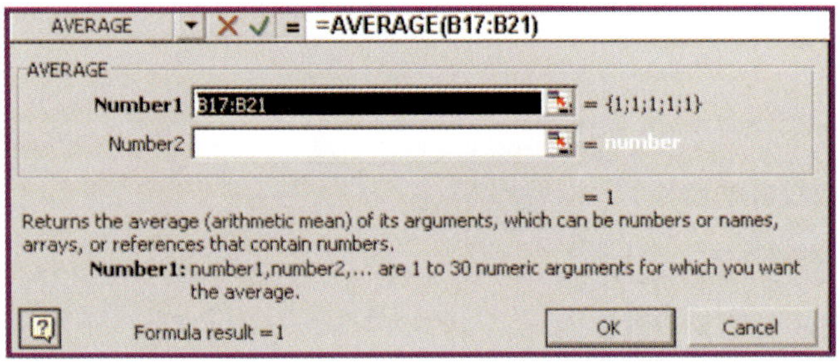

AppleWorks

9. Select cells B17:B22.
10. Choose **Auto Average** from the **Calculate** menu.

Cell B22 should have the number 1. This is Jess's daily average.

Bernie's Typing Activities

Key each drill line twice; key each paragraph once.

Reinforce: q, ?, z, tab

all letters learned

1 exact above wrong hike jail dump safety

2 exact above wrong hike jail dump safety

q emphasis

3 acquit quickly quote quite quill acquire

4 acquit quickly quote quite quill acquire

? (question mark)

5 Is it? What? When? Where? Why? How?

6 Is it? What? When? Where? Why? How?

z emphasis

7 zoo zap zone zoom zinc ritzy jazzy dozen

8 zoo zap zone zoom zinc ritzy jazzy dozen

tab emphasis

9 tab→ Jack tab→ Sam tab→ Jan tab→ Kay tab→ Mark

10 tab→ Jack tab→ Sam tab→ Jan tab→ Kay tab→ Mark

paragraphs

The space bar is used about every fifth or sixth stroke. You can increase your speed by using good technique when striking the space bar.

Keep the thumb low over the space bar. Move the thumb down and in quickly toward your palm.

3. Click on cell D6 and drag to D11.
4. With the cells still selected, click on the **Autosum** button on the toolbar.
5. Save your work.

Quick Check

Excellent! Check the totals in row 11. Are they the same as the ones shown below? If not, make your changes now.

	A	B	C	D	E	F	G	H	I
1				Professor Keys' Lab - Computer Use					
2									
3									
4	Number of hours used weekly								
5		Jess	Bernie	Jake					
6	Monday	1	3	2					
7	Tuesday	1	2	2					
8	Wednesday	1	1	2					
9	Thursday	1	2	2					
10	Friday	1	2	2					
11	Total Hours	5	10	10					

PART 5

Figuring Averages

You are doing a great job! Now let's create a new table to calculate the average amount of time Jess, Bernie, and Jake spend using the computers each day.

We will create a separate table to calculate the daily average.

1. Select cells A4:D11.
2. Click on the **Copy** button.
3. Click on cell A15.
4. Click on the **Paste** button.

Side Trips with Blueberry and Jess

Language Arts

Write The Patriots sent many messages to each other, all of which had to be kept secret from the British. Some messages were probably in code. Work with a partner to create your own secret code. Use a word processor. Use the code to write a message about the Boston Tea Party. For example, you might warn other Patriots to get ready for the event on December 16, 1773. E-mail the message to your classmates and see if they can break the code.

Social Studies

Research What do you know about tea? Where did it come from? Why was it so valuable in 1773? Use the Internet to find information. Copy the information into a word processing file. Then write a brief report. Be sure to use your own words and to cite your Internet source. Try to include information on the role of women in the boycott of tea that eventually led to the Boston Tea Party.

*If you need help citing a source, go to bensguide.gpo.gov. Click on **Help** at the bottom of the page. Click on the **How to Cite Ben's Guide** link. This page will show you how to cite your source.*

PART 4

Add Up the Hours

How many hours did Jess, Bernie, and Jake use the computer? Our spreadsheet can do the addition for us. Most spreadsheets have an Autosum button on the toolbar. It may look like this. Σ

To use the Autosum button, you must select a range of cells that are next to each other. We want to select the range of cells B6 to B11. The sum will go in cell B11.

1. Click on cell B6.
2. Drag the mouse to cell B11.
3. Click on the **Autosum** button on the toolbar.

The Autosum command uses an addition formula to add the numbers in cells B6–B10. The answer is in cell B11. The formula is displayed in the formula bar at the top of the spreadsheet.

The formula appears in the formula bar.

The total appears here.

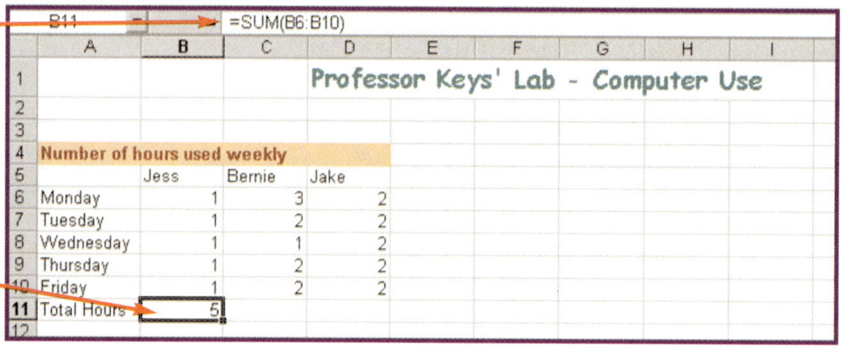

B11 =SUM(B6:B10)

	A	B	C	D	E	F	G	H	I
1				Professor Keys' Lab - Computer Use					
2									
3									
4	Number of hours used weekly								
5		Jess	Bernie	Jake					
6	Monday	1	3	2					
7	Tuesday	1	2	2					
8	Wednesday	1	1	2					
9	Thursday	1	2	2					
10	Friday	1	2	2					
11	Total Hours	5							
12									

Now let's get the totals for Bernie and Jake.

1. Click on cell C6 and drag to cell C11.
2. With the cells still selected, click on the **Autosum** button on the toolbar.

Project 8

Word Processing

Read All About It!

In this project you will:

- Insert a date
- Set page orientation
- Set margins
- Create columns
- Insert a graphic

Word Power

banner

column

Landscape orientation

margin

PART 3

Time Well Spent

Great! You are getting the hang of it. Now let's enter the data for Bernie and Jake. Use the numbers in my notepad.

	Jess	Bernie	Jake
Monday	1	3	2
Tuesday	1	2	2
Wednesday	1	1	2
Thursday	1	2	2
Friday	1	2	2

1. Click on cell C6. Type *3*.

Continue entering Bernie's hours in column C.

Good work! Now let's enter Jake's hours.

2. Click on cell D6. Type *2*.

Continue entering Jake's hours in column D.

3. Save the file again.

Quick Check

Nice work! The spreadsheet should look like this. Check your work now.

	A	B	C	D	E	F	G	H	I
1				Professor Keys' Lab - Computer Use					
2									
3									
4	Number of hours used weekly								
5		Jess	Bernie	Jake					
6	Monday	1	3	2					
7	Tuesday	1	2	2					
8	Wednesday	1	1	2					
9	Thursday	1	2	2					
10	Friday	1	2	2					
11	Total Hours								

Project 8

Design the Front Page of a Newspaper

I hope you are enjoying learning about the Patriots! I found out that Ben Franklin once published a newspaper called the Pennsylvania Gazette. *It made me think that my article about the Boston Tea Party could appear in a newspaper.*

Let's call our newspaper the Boston Gazette. *We will need a* **banner***, which gives the name of the newspaper and the date in big, bold letters. The article will go in two* **columns***. We will also insert a graphic. Let's get started on the first edition of the* Boston Gazette!

PART 1

Banner Basics

Let's open my article about the Boston Tea Party. Together we will create a banner.

1. Open the file named *gazette*.
2. Choose **Save As** from the **File** menu.
3. Name the file *gazette8*.
4. Put your cursor at the top of the page.
5. Type ***Boston Gazette***.

2. Jess used the computer for 1 hour on Tuesday. Click on cell B7 and type *1*.
3. On Wednesday, Jess used the computer for 1 hour. Click on cell B8 and type *1*.
4. On Thursday, Jess used the computer for 1 hour. Click on cell B9 and type *1*.
5. On Friday, Jess used the computer for 1 hour. Click on cell B10 and type *1*.
6. Save your work.

Quick Check

Excellent! The spreadsheet should look like this. Check your work now.

	A	B	C	D	E	F	G	H	I
1				Professor Keys' Lab - Computer Use					
2									
3									
4	Number of hours used weekly								
5		Jess	Bernie	Jake					
6	Monday	1							
7	Tuesday	1							
8	Wednesday	1							
9	Thursday	1							
10	Friday	1							
11	Total Hours								

Jake's Ergonomics Tip

When you work at the computer, take short exercise breaks. Every half hour, stand up and stretch. Gently shake your wrists. Make circles with your shoulders. First circle your shoulders forward. Then stop and circle them in the opposite direction.

Now have fun adding some style to your banner.

6. Select the words ***Boston Gazette*** and choose an interesting font and a large font size.
7. Center the words and click on the **Bold** button.

Most newspapers use a standard format for the date that spells out the day and month: Monday, April 19, 2004.

8. Place the cursor where you want the date to appear.

Word

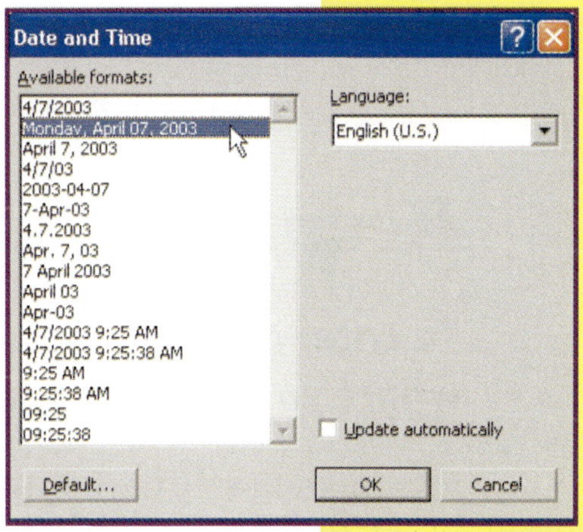

Word

9. Choose **Date and Time** from the **Insert** menu.
10. Choose the style you want, and click on **OK**.
11. Center the date.
12. Save your work.

AppleWorks

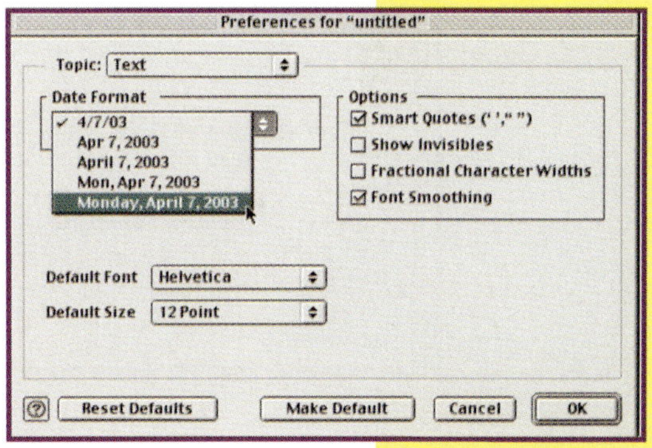

AppleWorks

9. Choose **Preferences** from the **Edit** menu, then choose **General**.
10. Click on the down arrow in the box under **Date Format**.
11. Choose the style you want, and click on **OK**.
12. Choose **Insert Date** from the **Edit** menu. Then choose **Fixed**.
13. Center the date.
14. Save your work.

Quick Check

Here is what my banner looks like.

Boston Gazette

Monday, April 9, 2004

Let's open my spreadsheet file. Then we will save the file with a new name.

1. Open your spreadsheet program.
2. Open the file *computer*.
3. Choose **Save As** from the **File** menu.
4. Name the file *computer13.*

PART 2

Keeping Track of Time

To enter data in a spreadsheet, just click on the cells where you want to put the data.

1. Jess used the computer for 1 hour on Monday. Click on cell B6 and type *1*.

	A	B	C	D	E	F	G	H	I
1				Professor Keys' Lab - Computer Use					
2									
3									
4	Number of hours used weekly								
5		Jess	Bernie	Jake					
6	Monday	1							
7	Tuesday								
8	Wednesday								
9	Thursday								
10	Friday								
11	Total Hours								

PART 2

Front Page Focus

Because most newspapers are set in columns, we will put the article into two columns. First, let's set the margins and set up the page with Landscape orientation.

Word

1. Choose **Page Setup** from the **File** menu.

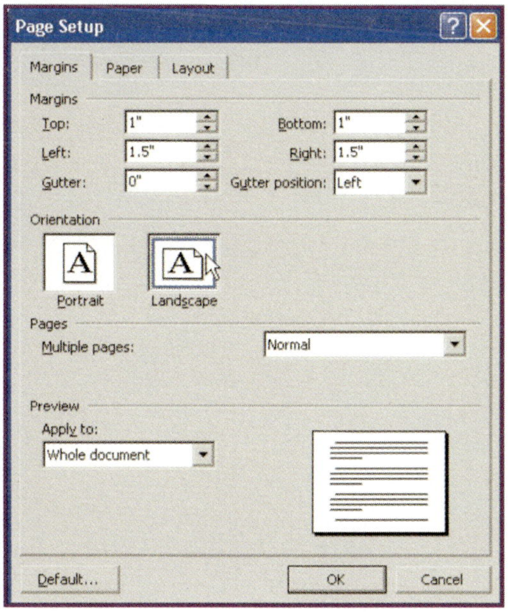

AppleWorks

1. Choose **Document** from the **Format** menu.

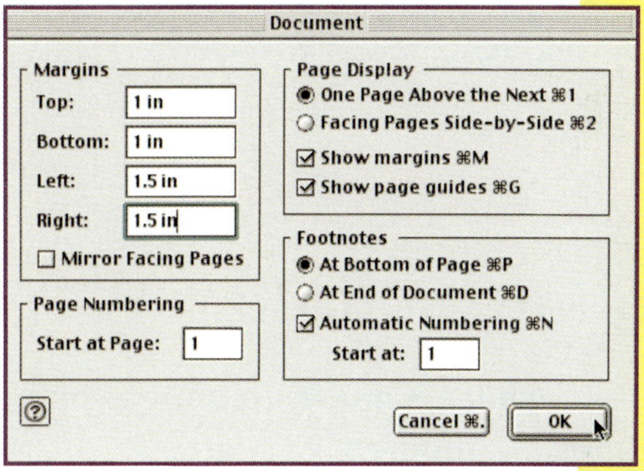

2. Place your cursor in the **Top** box and type *1"*.
3. Move to the **Bottom** box and type *1"*.
4. Move to the **Left** box and type *1.5"*.
5. Move to the **Right** box and type *1.5"*.
6. Select **Landscape** in the orientation box.
7. Click **OK**.

*AppleWorks users must choose **Page Setup** from the **File** menu to select the Landscape orientation.*

Project 13

Use a Spreadsheet to Figure Averages

My computer lab is a busy place. Bernie, Jake, and Jess are always using the computers, and everybody else has to wait! I think I may need to buy more computers.

*I will use a **spreadsheet** to keep track of how many hours a week Jess, Bernie, and Jake use the computers. I will also figure out how many hours a day, on **average**, they use the computers. I have already set up the spreadsheet and entered some of the data. Let's enter the rest of the data for Bernie, Jess, and Jake together!*

PART 1

Getting Started

*A spreadsheet is made up of **rows** and **columns**. The columns are labeled with letters. The rows are labeled with numbers. A spreadsheet can help you add, subtract, multiply, and divide. It can also help you calculate averages.*

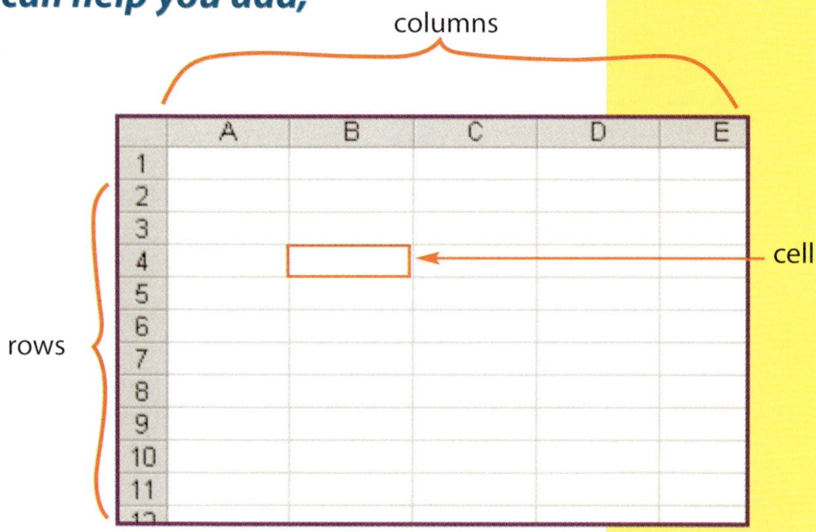

Now let's create two columns. It is so easy.

Word

1. Select the article title and all of the text.
2. Choose **Columns** from the **Format** menu.
3. Click on the picture that shows two columns.
4. Click on **OK**.

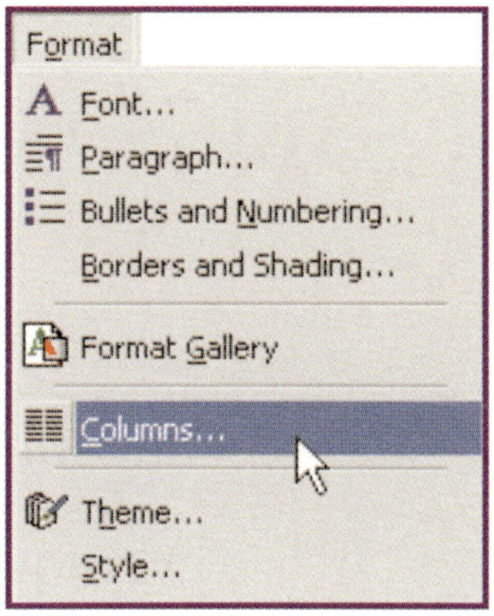

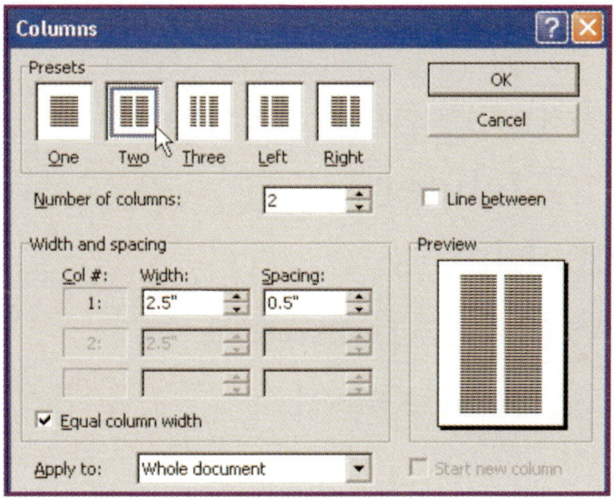

You can also click on the ***Columns*** *button on the toolbar.*

Jake's Ergonomics Tip

Every 15 minutes or so, you should look away from the screen for a moment. Blink your eyes quickly a few times to relax your eye muscles. This activity also has another benefit: You get a "fresh view" of your work when you look at it again!

Project 13

Spreadsheet

Figure It Out

In this project you will:

- Enter data in a spreadsheet
- Use a spreadsheet to solve problems
- Use the Average formula
- Format a spreadsheet
- Add charts

Word Power

Autosum

average

chart

column

formula

function

legend

range

row

spreadsheet

AppleWorks

1. Put your cursor on the next line under your banner.
2. Choose **Insert Section Break** from the **Format** menu.
3. Click on the **Increase Columns** control button on your toolbar.

4. Click so that the number *2* appears.
5. Save your work.

You may need to adjust the two columns so that they balance, or have the same amount of copy.

1. Place your cursor where you want the columns to break.

Word

2. Choose **Break** from the **Insert** menu.
3. Click on **Column Break.**

AppleWorks

2. Choose **Insert Column Break** from the **Format** menu.

Word

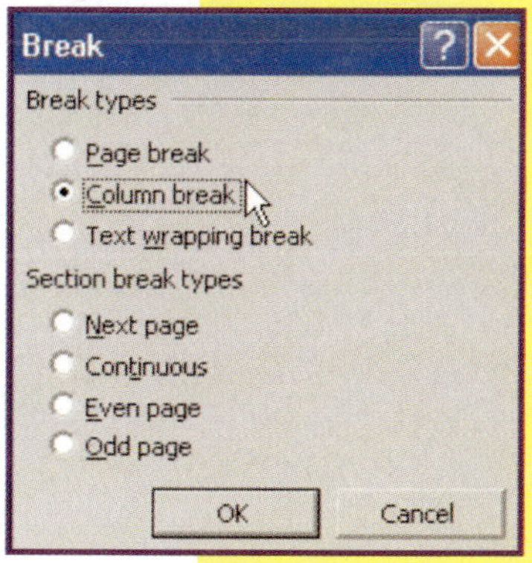

Quick Check

I told you it was easy! Your article should now be set in two columns. If not, try the steps again.

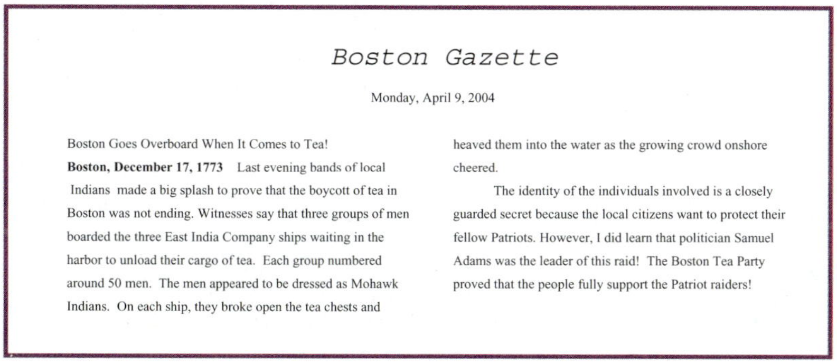
Boston Gazette

Monday, April 9, 2004

Boston Goes Overboard When It Comes to Tea!

Boston, December 17, 1773 Last evening bands of local Indians made a big splash to prove that the boycott of tea in Boston was not ending. Witnesses say that three groups of men boarded the three East India Company ships waiting in the harbor to unload their cargo of tea. Each group numbered around 50 men. The men appeared to be dressed as Mohawk Indians. On each ship, they broke open the tea chests and heaved them into the water as the growing crowd onshore cheered.

The identity of the individuals involved is a closely guarded secret because the local citizens want to protect their fellow Patriots. However, I did learn that politician Samuel Adams was the leader of this raid! The Boston Tea Party proved that the people fully support the Patriot raiders!

Side Trips with Blueberry and Jess

Social Studies

Create Create a slide show about the Statue of Liberty. How and when did it get to the United States? Who is Emma Lazarus, and what does she have to do with the statue? One good Web site to check is http://www.nps.gov/stli. You can also use a reference CD-ROM. Add a graphic of the Statue of Liberty in your slide show.

Language Arts

Create Find out about our national anthem, "The Star-Spangled Banner." Find out who wrote it, when, and why. Did you know that we only sing one verse of this song? Create a slide show about the history of this song. Add a recording of the song onto one of your slides.

PART 3

A Worthy Picture

A picture is worth a thousand words. Let's insert a graphic of Samuel Adams or a Boston Tea Party ship.

1. Put your cursor where you want the graphic to go.

Word

2. Choose **Picture** from the **Insert** menu.

AppleWorks

2. Choose **Insert** from the **File** menu.

3. Insert your graphic.

You may need to adjust the columns again so that they balance. Look back at Part 2.

4. Save your work.

Use the sizing handles to make the graphic bigger or smaller to fit the column.

Quick Check

Excellent work! Your newspaper article should look something like this.

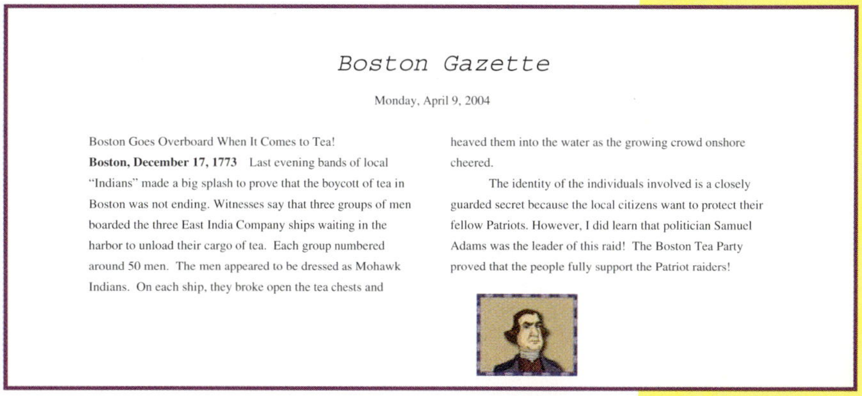

Boston Gazette

Monday, April 9, 2004

Boston Goes Overboard When It Comes to Tea!

Boston, December 17, 1773 Last evening bands of local "Indians" made a big splash to prove that the boycott of tea in Boston was not ending. Witnesses say that three groups of men boarded the three East India Company ships waiting in the harbor to unload their cargo of tea. Each group numbered around 50 men. The men appeared to be dressed as Mohawk Indians. On each ship, they broke open the tea chests and heaved them into the water as the growing crowd onshore cheered.

The identity of the individuals involved is a closely guarded secret because the local citizens want to protect their fellow Patriots. However, I did learn that politician Samuel Adams was the leader of this raid! The Boston Tea Party proved that the people fully support the Patriot raiders!

On Your Own

Improve your page by changing the font and font size of the article title.

Bernie's Typing Activities

Key each drill line twice; key each paragraph once.

Reinforce 9 & 4

1. Only 9 of the 94 boys ran the next race.
2. Zack and I were married on May 14, 1994.
3. Jane was born on May 14, 1994, at 9 a.m.
4. The 94 men met on May 19, 1998, at 8 p.m.
5. Was their copyright 1849, 1949, or 1994?

Who Am I?

I am known for quite a few things. Perhaps you know me for leading a brave army across the Delaware on Christmas night.

Perhaps you know me as the Commander in Chief of the Continental Army. Perhaps you know me as the first President of the United States. Who am I?

Bernie's Typing Activities

Open your word processor. Key the drill lines.

Review

a/b

1 Aaron and Barb fibbed about being broke.

c/d

2 Cody and Zac divided the dividend check.

e/f

3 Frank offered to take three percent off.

g/h

4 He gave her half of the eight gold eggs.

i/j

5 Joni and Jim will join the jury in June.

k/l

6 Lillian left the knickknack in the hall.

m/n

7 The minimum amount may be needed sooner.

o/p

8 Ron Opal opened the box of four puppies.

q/r

9 Barbara quite quickly quoted Dr. Robert.

s/t

10 Steve said he trusts Tess to start fast.

u/v

11 Vivacious Vivian left unusually subdued.

w/x

12 The six tax experts will work two weeks.

y/z

13 Dizzy, hazy, and crazy are all zy words.

PART 7

Strike Up the Band

Patriotic music really stirs the emotions! Let's get the audience in the patriotic spirit. Add sound to Slide 1.

1. Click on Slide 1.

PowerPoint

2. Choose **Movies and Sounds** from the **Insert** menu. Then choose **Sound from Files**.
3. Find the file ***patriotic music***.
4. Click **Insert**.

AppleWorks

2. Choose **Insert** from the **File** menu.
3. Find the file ***patriotic music***.
4. Drag it onto Slide 1.

A speaker icon will appear on Slide 1. Drag it to the corner so that it is not in the way.

5. To play the sound, double-click on it.
6. Run the slide show.
7. Save your work.

You did it—what a fabulous show, full of good information, pictures, and sound!

On Your Own

Add another slide to your slide show. Use the Internet to find out about the Liberty Bell. Add clip art to your slide.

Side Trips with Blueberry and Jess

Language Arts

Design With a partner, make a list of household items that colonists might buy. Then choose one item and design an ad for it that will go in your newspaper. Choose an interesting font and style for the words. Insert a graphic of the item.

Math

Calculate Develop a business plan to sell your newspaper. How much will you charge for each copy? How much does it cost to print the newspaper? Figure out how many copies you must sell to make a profit. Type your plan in a list. Use two columns. Use headings in your business plan so that the reader can understand your facts and figures easily.

4. Click on the **Automatically after** box to advance each slide automatically.
5. Type *20* or use the arrow to set the number of seconds each slide will be displayed.
6. Click on **Apply to All Slides**.
7. Save your work.

AppleWorks

1. Click on the **Slide** tab in the **Controls** window. 
2. Select Slide 1.
3. Choose *Box* from the pull-down menu.
4. Then repeat steps 2 and 3 to apply the transition to slides 2, 3, 4, and 5.
5. Click on the **Slide Show** tab in the **Controls** window. 
6. Click on **Auto-advance every** and type *20*.
7. Save your work.

PowerPoint

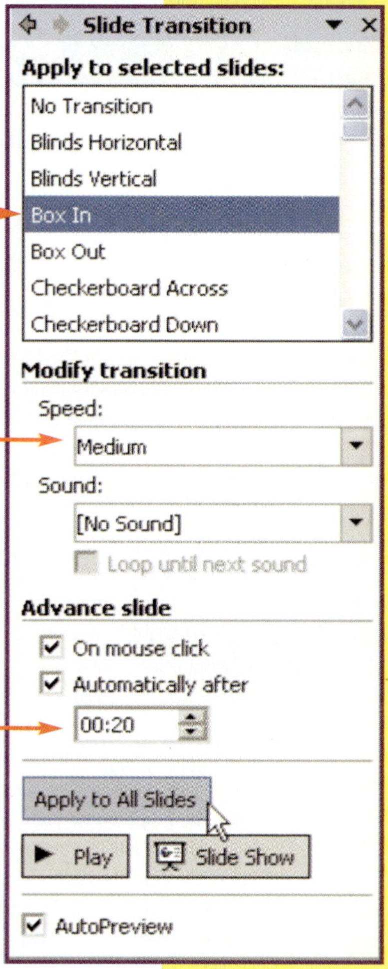

Name of the transition

Speed of the transition

Interval between advance of slides

AppleWorks

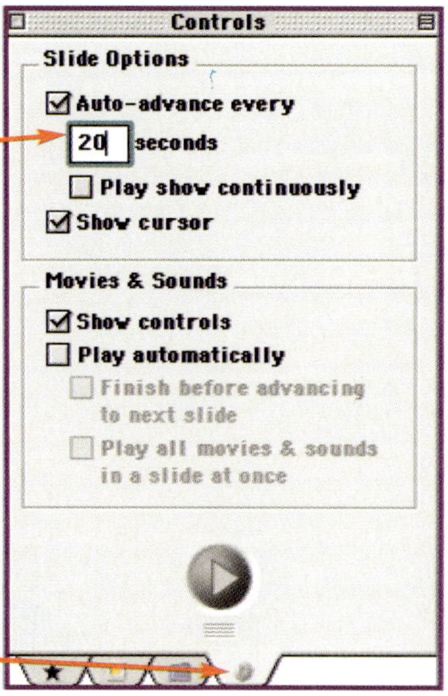

Click to automatically advance the slides.

Slide Show tab

Run your slide show after you have added transitions and timing to see how well they work.

Project 9

Internet and Word Processing

Colonial Workers

In this project you will:

- Use electronic reference tools
- Multitask between two open programs
- Cite a source
- Format a document
- Set text in three columns
- Use the spelling checker

Word Power

cite

column

PART 5

Cite Your Sources

Hurray! You are on the last slide. Now we will list where we found our information. Always cite your sources.

1. Add a new slide or click on Slide 5.
2. Click on the title box and type ***Sources***.
3. Click on or create a text box and type your sources. Here is where I found my facts:

   Teresa Bateman, *Red, White, Blue, and Uncle Who? The Story Behind Some of America's Patriotic Symbols,* Holiday House Books, 2001.
4. Save the slide show.

You have done it! Five great slides are almost ready for presentation.

PART 6

Add Some Fireworks

Let's add visual interest by choosing a transition between slides. Some slides fade out as the next ones come in. Let's choose a transition for our slides. We can also set how many seconds each slide will be displayed.

PowerPoint

1. Choose **Slide Transition** from the **Slide Show** menu.
2. Click on ***Box In***.
3. To set the timing, click on the drop-down arrow in the **Speed** box and choose **Medium**.

Project 9

Revise a Report

Hi! I am back home now after traveling back in time to colonial America. People in those days sure had to work hard. Some of their jobs were very different from those we have today. You don't see too many blacksmiths today, but in colonial times they were important. I am writing a report about colonial life in the 1700s. I hope you enjoy reading it! I need to add some more information to my report. Then I will make sure my report is in the proper format. Will you help me?

PART 1

A Work in Progress

Let's open my report. Our first job will be to find some facts to add to it. You can use an encyclopedia on the Internet or an encyclopedia on a CD-ROM to search for the facts.

1. Open the file named *work*.
2. Choose **Save As** from the **File** menu.
3. Name the file *work9*.

3. Click on the next text box or create a text box in AppleWorks, and type *In the War of 1812, Sam Wilson sold meat to the U.S. Army. Wilson's nickname was Uncle Sam. The boxes were stamped with the letters U.S. So when someone asked what the letters U.S. stood for, Wilson's workers joked that they stood for Uncle Sam.*
4. Save your work.

You can add a piece of clip art of Uncle Sam if you like. Slide 3 may look like this.

Slide 3

PART 4

Our National Emblem

The national emblem of the United States is the bald eagle. On Slide 4, let's explain how it came to be our emblem.

Check your spelling!

1. Add a new slide, or click on Slide 4.
2. Click on the title box and type *The Bald Eagle*.
3. Click on or create the next text box and type *The bald eagle is our national emblem. Ben Franklin wanted the turkey because it was a useful domestic bird. But Congress didn't think the turkey was impressive enough. Congress chose the bald eagle instead. The bald eagle is found only in North America.*
4. Save the slide show.

Very good! Slide 4 should look like this. You can add clip art, too!

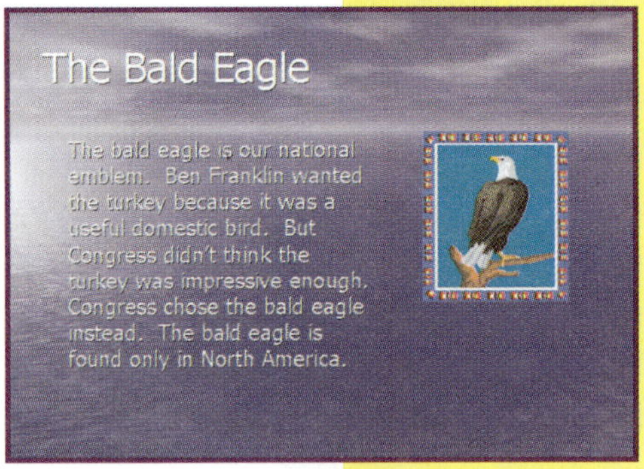

Slide 4

In the first paragraph, I mention the middle colonies, but I don't name them. Adding the names of these middle colonies in parentheses will add some good details to my report.

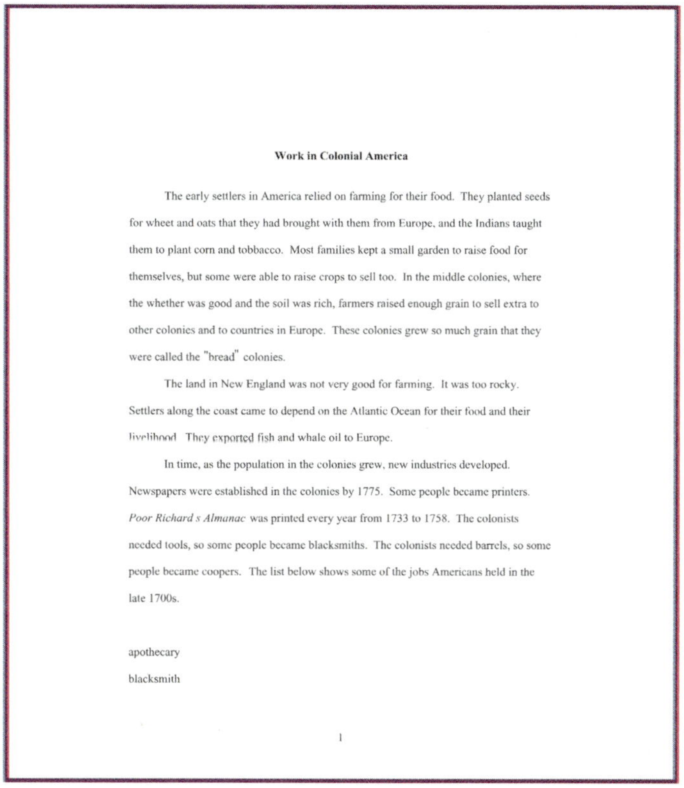

Work in Colonial America

The early settlers in America relied on farming for their food. They planted seeds for wheat and oats that they had brought with them from Europe, and the Indians taught them to plant corn and tobbacco. Most families kept a small garden to raise food for themselves, but some were able to raise crops to sell too. In the middle colonies, where the whether was good and the soil was rich, farmers raised enough grain to sell extra to other colonies and to countries in Europe. These colonies grew so much grain that they were called the "bread" colonies.

The land in New England was not very good for farming. It was too rocky. Settlers along the coast came to depend on the Atlantic Ocean for their food and their livelihood. They exported fish and whale oil to Europe.

In time, as the population in the colonies grew, new industries developed. Newspapers were established in the colonies by 1775. Some people became printers. *Poor Richard s Almanac* was printed every year from 1733 to 1758. The colonists needed tools, so some people became blacksmiths. The colonists needed barrels, so some people became coopers. The list below shows some of the jobs Americans held in the late 1700s.

apothecary

blacksmith

1

I used the World Book Encyclopedia CD-ROM. You can use another reference CD-ROM or online encyclopedia.

4. Open your reference CD-ROM or your Internet browser program.
5. If you are using an online encyclopedia, navigate to that Web site now.
6. In the Search box, type ***middle colonies***.

PART 2

It's a Grand Old Flag

My next slide tells about the American flag.

PowerPoint

1. Click on the **New Slide** button. Choose the **Title + Text** layout.

AppleWorks

1. Click on Slide 2.

2. In the slide's title box, type *The Flag*.
3. Click on the next text box or bullet. Type *The 13 stripes stand for the 13 original colonies*.
4. Click on the next text box or bullet. Type *Each star stands for a state*.
5. Insert clip art of the flag. Click and drag your clip art to position it on the slide.
6. Save the file.

Slide 2

In AppleWorks, delete two of the bullets before typing the text in Step 3.

PART 3

Uncle Sam Wants You!

Now let's tell about Uncle Sam. Who was Uncle Sam?

PowerPoint

1. Click on the **New Slide** button. Choose the **Title + Text** layout.

AppleWorks

1. Click on Slide 3.

2. Click on the title box and type *Uncle Sam.*

You should find a list of articles or links on your topic.

7. Click on a link to find the names of the middle colonies.
8. When you have found the names, navigate back to the file *work9*.
9. Place your cursor between the word *colonies* and the comma in sentence 4 of the first paragraph, and add the names in parentheses.

Quick Check

Did you type* New York, New Jersey, Pennsylvania, *and* Delaware? *Way to go! I knew you could do it!

***Now let's search for the person who wrote and published* Poor Richard's Almanac.**

10. Return to your encyclopedia.
11. Type the search words ***Poor Richard's Almanac***.
12. When you find the information you want, go back to the file *work9*.
13. Add the new information in paragraph 3 following the fourth sentence. Type the sentence ***The writer and publisher of this almanac was*** [add the name].
14. Save your work.

Quick Check

Did you type* Benjamin Franklin? *Super! Does your file look like this?

Work in Colonial America

The early settlers in America relied on farming for their food. They planted seeds for wheat and oats that they had brought with them from Europe, and the Indians taught them to plant corn and tobbacco. Most families kept a small garden to raise food for themselves, but some were able to raise crops to sell too. In the middle colonies (New York, New Jersey, Pennsylvania, and Delaware), where the whether was good and the soil was rich, farmers raised enough grain to sell extra to other colonies and to countries in Europe. These colonies grew so much grain that they were called the "bread" colonies.

The land in New England was not very good for farming. It was too rocky. Settlers along the coast came to depend on the Atlantic Ocean for their food and their livelihood. They exported fish and whale oil to Europe.

In time, as the population in the colonies grew, new industries developed. Newspapers were established in the colonies by 1775. Some people became printers. *Poor Richard's Almanac* was printed every year from 1733 to 1758. The writer and publisher of this almanac was Benjamin Franklin. The colonists needed tools, so some people became blacksmiths. The colonists needed barrels, so some people became coopers. The list below shows some of the jobs Americans held in the late 1700s.

AppleWorks

1. Open AppleWorks.
2. Click on the **Templates** tab.
3. Choose *Hip Presentation*.

Three slides have been created for you. You need to create two more.

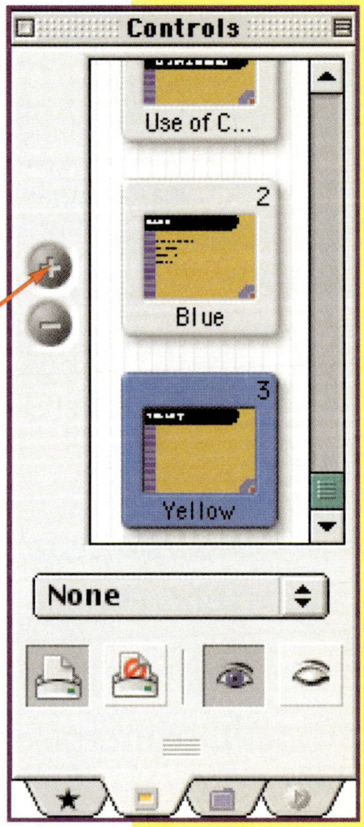

Click on the **Plus** (+) button.

4. To create Slide 4, click on Slide 3, and then click on the **Plus** (+) button.
5. Click on the **Plus** (+) button again to create one more slide.

Let's change the background to a shade of blue to match our theme.

6. Click on the text box in Slide 1.
7. Choose **Edit Background** from the **Options** menu.
8. Click on the **Color palette** button and choose a shade of blue.
9. Choose **Edit Background** again from the **Options** menu.
10. Save your slide show as *symbols12*.

Now let's enter the title of the slide show on Slide 1. In AppleWorks, first select the text and then type your title.

1. Click on Slide 1.
2. Click on the title box. Type *Patriotic Symbols of America*.
3. Save the file again.

Your slide may look like this.

Slide 1

A good start—now let's move on.

PART 2

Whose Words?

My report includes facts and dates. I need to tell, or cite, the source of the information.

1. Navigate to the first article in the reference CD-ROM or the Web page that you used to research the middle colonies.
2. Scroll down to the end of the article to find the source.
3. Copy the source of your information.
4. Navigate back to the file ***work9***.
5. Put your cursor at the end of the file.
6. Paste the information.
7. Save your work.

Your source should give, in this order, the author, the name of the article, and the name of the encyclopedia.

If you paste text from the Internet, you will have to change the font and font size to match the rest of your file.

Quick Check

Your source information might look like this.

Joan R. Gundersen, "Colonial Life in America," *World Book Encyclopedia,* 2003, version 7.00.

source for encyclopedia on CD-ROM

Joan R. Gundersen, "Colonial Life in America," *World Book Online Americas Edition*, http://www.worldbookonline.com/ar?/na/ar/co/ar124100.htm, April 30, 2004.

source for online encyclopedia

***Follow the same steps above to cite the source where you learned who wrote* Poor Richard's Almanac.**

Project 12

Create a Patriotic Slide Show

My class is making a slide show of patriotic symbols in America. Of course, we start with the American flag! Uncle Sam is another symbol of the United States. Everyone recognizes Uncle Sam in his red, white, and blue clothes. We will explain how these symbols came to be and add graphics. We will also add some patriotic music. Let's do it together!

PART 1

A Patriotic Theme

Choose a template that matches the patriotic theme.

PowerPoint

1. Open PowerPoint.
2. Choose **New** from the **File** menu.
3. Click on **From Design Template** in the task pane (or click on the **Design Templates** tab).
4. Choose the *Oceans* template.
5. Save your slide show as *symbols12*.

Jake's Ergonomics Tip

Take a break and do shoulder rolls. Press your shoulders gently up to your ears, drop them down, and squeeze them together behind your back.

PART 3

A Closer Look

Now we can proofread the report. We can use the spelling checker to find errors in spelling. The spelling checker does not find all mistakes, however. A word can be spelled correctly but it can be the wrong word. We still need to read the report carefully.

1. Run the spelling checker.

***The spelling checker will highlight the word* wheet.**

2. Select the word *wheat* and click on **Change** or **Replace**.
3. Select the word *tobacco* and click on **Change** or **Replace**.
4. Click on **OK** or **Done**.
5. Find the word *whether* in paragraph 1.
6. Double-click on it and type *weather*.
7. Save your work.

Jake's Ergonomics Tip

Take a break and stretch. Place your right hand on your left shoulder. Then place your left hand on your right elbow and push it gently to the left and up slightly. Hold for a count of four. Repeat the stretch, this time with your left shoulder.

Project 12

Graphics and Multimedia

Uncle Sam

In this project you will:

- Create a slide show
- Use a template
- Cite sources
- Add transitions and timing
- Insert audio and graphics

Word Power

cite

timing

transition

PART 4

Set the Standards

My report should have one-inch margins. Like most reports, it should be set in Portrait orientation. Let's format the document now.

Word

1. Choose **Page Setup** from the **File** menu.
2. Set the top, bottom, left, and right margins to 1 inch.
3. Click on **Portrait** orientation.
4. Click on **OK**.

Your margins and page orientation may already be set, but you should always check them.

AppleWorks

1. Choose **Document** from the **Format** menu.
2. Set the top, bottom, left, and right margins at 1 inch.
3. Click on **OK**.
4. Choose **Page Setup** from the **File** menu.
5. Click on the **Portrait** orientation.
6. Click on **OK**.

My list of jobs takes up too many lines. I want to set that copy in three columns.

Word

1. Select the list of jobs, from ***apothecary*** through ***wig maker***.
2. Click on the **Columns** button.
3. Click on **3 Columns**.
4. Save your work.

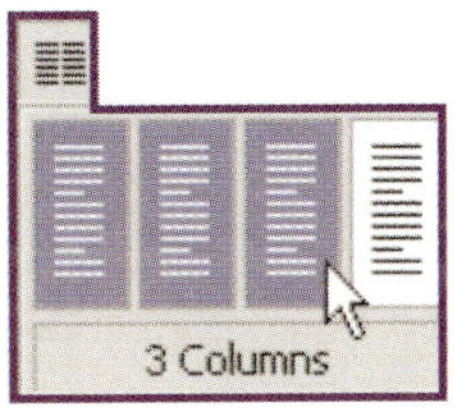

Side Trips with Blueberry and Jess

Science

Create Create a slide show about the life cycle of a frog or a butterfly. Use an encyclopedia on a CD-ROM or the Internet or your library to research your choice. Add a picture to at least one slide. Why not draw a picture and scan it into your files? You can also insert clip art. Write a script to go with your slide show. Present your slide show to your classmates.

Language Arts

Create People, too, grow and change over the years. Collect some pictures of yourself or your family members. Scan those pictures into the computer. Then create a slide show that shows how you and your family have changed over time. You could record the voices of your family for this presentation, too. Use the Help feature of your presentation program if you need help.

AppleWorks

1. Put your cursor at the line of space above the list.
2. Choose **Insert Section Break** from the **Format** menu.
3. Put your cursor at the end of the list and tap **Return**.
4. Choose **Insert Section Break** from the **Format** menu.
5. Select all the words in the list.
6. Click on the **Increase columns** control button on the toolbar to show 3 columns.

7. Click at the end of *wigmaker* and choose **Insert Section Break** from the **Format** menu.
8. Save your work.

Quick Check

Page 2 of your report should look something like this.

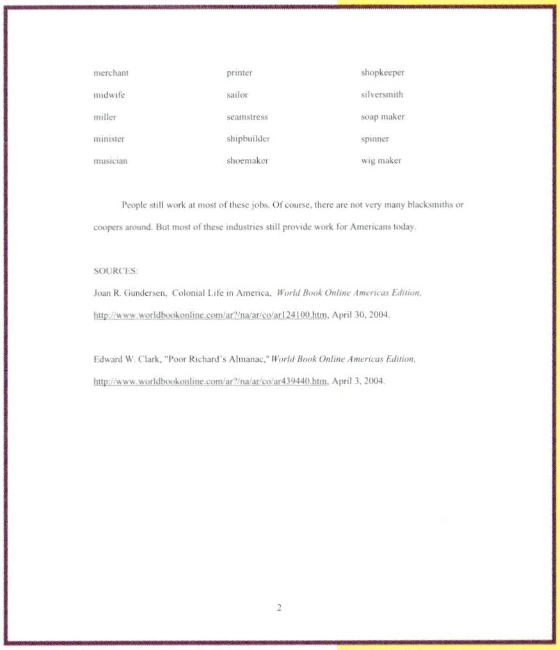

merchant	printer	shopkeeper
midwife	sailor	silversmith
miller	seamstress	soap maker
minister	shipbuilder	spinner
musician	shoemaker	wig maker

People still work at most of these jobs. Of course, there are not very many blacksmiths or coopers around. But most of these industries still provide work for Americans today.

SOURCES:

Joan R. Gundersen, Colonial Life in America, *World Book Online Americas Edition*, http://www.worldbookonline.com/ar?/na/ar/co/ar124100.htm, April 30, 2004.

Edward W. Clark, "Poor Richard's Almanac," *World Book Online Americas Edition*, http://www.worldbookonline.com/ar?/na/ar/co/ar439440.htm, April 3, 2004.

2

On Your Own

Return to the encyclopedia you used to research the middle colonies. Find one more piece of information you can add to the report.

Bernie's Typing Activities

Key each drill line twice; key each paragraph once.

Reinforce: 8 & 1

1. I added 18 and 81. She added 18 and 18.
2. Key the figures 1, 81, 18, 181, and 811.
3. They had 18 goats, 81 ducks, and 8 pigs.
4. Was the date June 1, June 8, or June 18?
5. Did 81 of the 818 members take the test?

Who Am I?

I live in Missouri with my Aunt Polly. I hide in the closet when I'm in trouble. Because I like to pull pranks on people, I am in trouble quite often.

I grew up in a river town. My girl friend is Becky Thatcher. I like excitement and adventures and quite often find myself in amazingly dangerous situations. Who am I?

Bernie's Typing Activities

Key each drill line twice; key each paragraph once.

Skill Building

balanced-hand sentences

1. Jay and I may work for the city auditor.
2. Pamela may make six vivid signs to hang.
3. Helen may handle the audit for the firm.
4. Eight of the firms may bid on the signs.
5. Jana and Alan may cycle to the big lake.

Timed writings/paragraphs

. 2 . 4 . 6 . 8 . 10
Learning to key requires a lot of work. If you do
. 12 . 14 . 16 . 18 .
the work, you will soon be amazed at how much
20 . 22 . 24 .
faster you will be able to key.

. 2 . 4 . 6 . 8 .
Work done at the computer is easier to read than
10 . 12 . 14 . 16 . 18 .
work done by hand. Also, corrections made at the
20 . 22 . 24 . 26 . 28
computer are easier to make and neater than
. 30 . 32 .
corrections done by hand.

AppleWorks

1. Click on Slide 4 in the **Controls** window.
2. Drag it after Slide 1 and drop it there.
3. Save the file.

AppleWorks

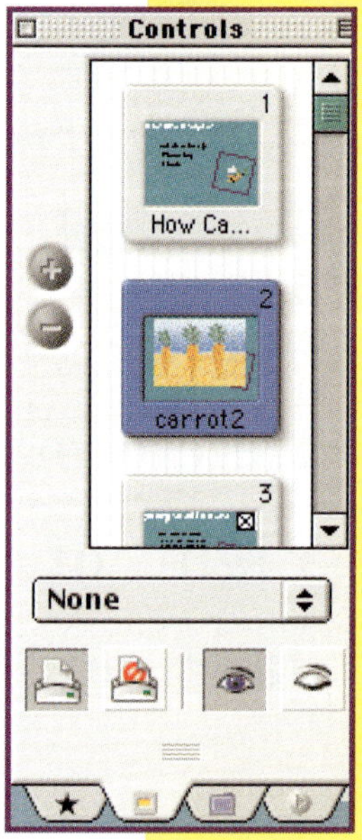

Let's see the result of all our hard work. Get ready to sit back and enjoy the show!

PowerPoint

1. Choose **Slide Show** from the **View** menu, or click on the **Slide Show** button in the lower left-hand corner of the window.
2. After the show has run, tap the **Escape** key to exit the slide show.

AppleWorks

1. Choose **Slide Show** from the **Window** menu. You can also click on the **Start Show** button on the toolbar.
2. After the show has run, tap the **Escape** key to exit the slide show.

Take a bow! You now have a wonderful way to teach your classmates about plants!

On Your Own

Change the transition to your slides. You can even add a different transition to each slide. Which one do you like best?

Side Trips with Blueberry and Jess

Social Studies

Research Paul Revere was a famous patriot in Boston. He was also a famous silversmith. Many of his bowls and tea servers are in museums. Design an infographic about Paul Revere that describes the important events in his life and shows at least one picture of him and one picture of his work. Search the Internet for information and pictures, and cite your sources.

Social Studies

Research What did people eat in colonial times? Use the Internet, an encyclopedia on a CD-ROM, or books from your school library to research this topic. Use search words such as *colonial America* or *daily life in colonial times*. Write your report on the word processor. Be sure to cite your sources. Add clip art to your report. If you find a recipe, try making it for your class.

PART 7

All in Good Order

I am writing a script to go with my slide show. I need to change the order of my slides to match my script. I want Slide 4 to come after Slide 1. Will you help me move this slide? Then we will run the slide show.

*You can also click on the **Slide Sorter** button in the lower left-hand corner of the window.*

PowerPoint

1. Choose **Slide Sorter** from the **View** menu.
2. Click on Slide 4.
3. Drag it after Slide 1 and drop it there.
4. Save the file.

PowerPoint

Jake's Ergonomics Tip

Time for a break after all that work! Try this exercise to help you sit up straight. Sit up straight and raise your arms above your head. Now clasp your hands and gently bring them down to touch the top of your head. Stretch them up again, and repeat this move several times. You can also use this stretch to take a break from doing homework.

Project 10

Graphics and Multimedia

The Timeline

In this project you will:

- Use design and layout skills
- Use draw tools
- Add text to a timeline

Word Power

Landscape orientation

text box

text frame

timeline

Now you must make three choices. What kind of transition would you like? How fast do you want the transition to occur? How long do you want each slide to be displayed?

2. Choose the slide transition ***Shape Plus***.
3. Use the drop-down arrow in the **Speed** box to choose **Medium**.
4. Click the box **Automatically after** and type ***10*** to set the time each slide is displayed.
5. Click on **Apply to All Slides**.
6. Run the slide show.
7. Save your work.

Name of the transition

Speed of the transition

Interval between advance of slides

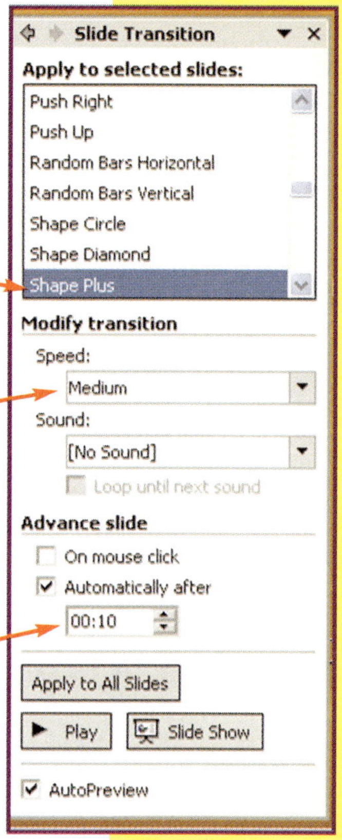

AppleWorks

1. Click on the **Slide** tab in the **Controls** window.
2. Click on the ***Barn Door*** transition from the list.
3. To apply the transition to the rest of your slides, repeat step 2 for each slide.
4. Click on the **Slide Show** tab in the **Controls** window to set the timing.
5. Click **Auto-advance every** and type ***10*** for the number of seconds you want between slides.
6. Run the slide show.
7. Save your work.

Did you like your transitions? You can change your settings.

Click on the *Barn Door* transition.

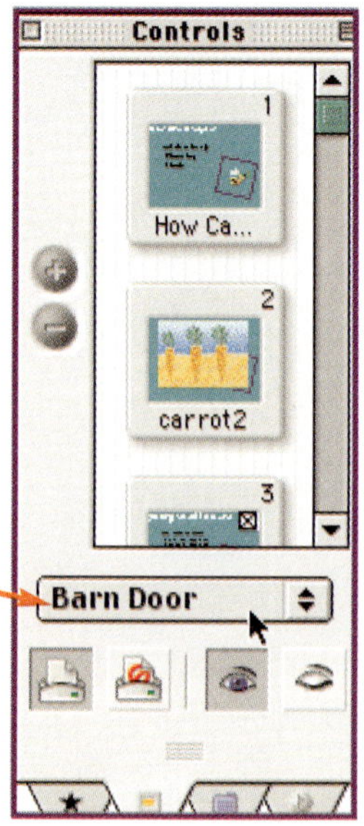

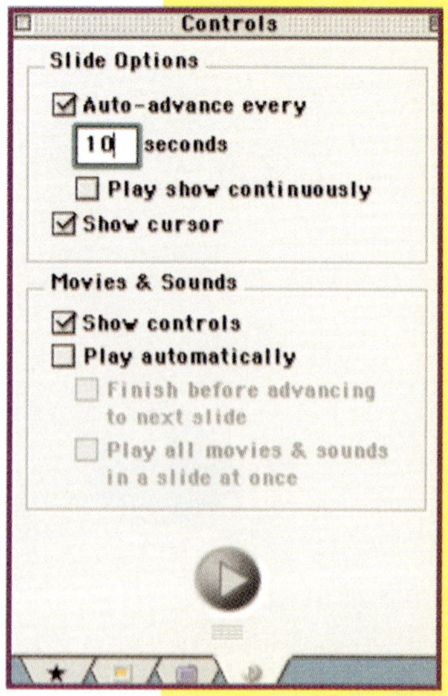

Create a Timeline of Thomas Edison's Inventions

I have used the Time Machine to go back to the year 1900 to talk to Thomas Alva Edison. He was one of America's most famous inventors. I want to put four of his major inventions on a timeline. A timeline will show at a glance what he invented and when he invented it.

PART 1

Set Up the Timeline

A timeline can go vertically down a page, or it can go horizontally across the page. Let's make a horizontal timeline. We will use Landscape orientation.

1. Create a new file.
2. Save it as *timeline10*.
3. Choose **Page Setup** from the **File** menu.
4. Click on the **Landscape** orientation.
5. Click **OK** to close.
6. Place your cursor at the top of the page.
7. Type the title *Thomas Alva Edison's Inventions*.

PART 5

To Your Health!

Let's add more facts about carrots on Slide 5.

1. Add a new slide in PowerPoint, or click on Slide 5 in AppleWorks.
2. Click in the title box. Type ***Carrots: The Root of Good Health***.
3. Click in the next box or bullet and type ***Carrots are vegetables because they are flowering plants. People eat the roots of the plant, which grow underground***.
4. Click in the next box or bullet and type ***Carrots contain beta carotene, a vitamin that is very good for your eyes.***
5. Save your work.

Slide 5

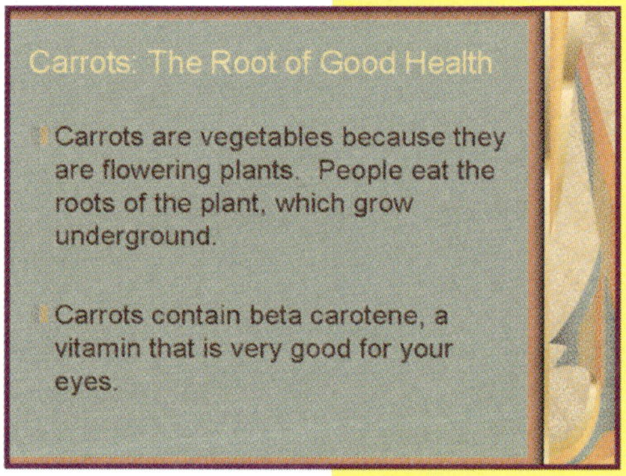

PART 6

Smooth Transitions

Let's decide now how the slide show will run. Instead of just turning off one slide and turning on the next, you can program the slides with transitions. A transition gradually changes one slide into another. We can change the transition, the speed of the transition, and the interval between each slide advance. Let's make these changes now.

PowerPoint

1. Choose **Slide Transition** from the **Slide Show** menu.

8. Select the title.
9. Click on the **Center** button to center it on the page.
10. Click again to place your cursor at the end of the title.
11. Tap the **Enter** key ten times so the cursor is closer to the middle of the page.

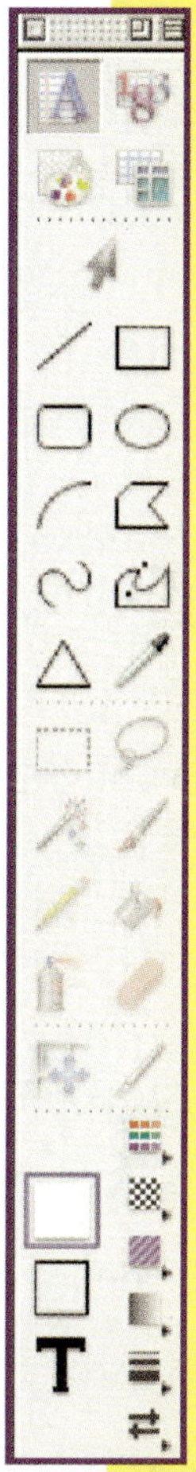

Now get ready to draw the horizontal timeline.

Word

12. Choose **Toolbars** from the **View** menu and select **Drawing.**

AppleWorks

12. Choose **Show Tools** from the **Window** menu.

13. Click on the **Line** button.

The cursor will look like this: +.

14. Draw a straight line all the way across the page. Hold down the **Shift** key to draw a straight line.
15. Tap **Enter** one time.
16. Save your work.

Jake's Ergonomics Tip

Give your eyes a rest. After working on the computer for 20 minutes, look at an object 20 feet away for 20 seconds.

PART 4

A New Layout

Our next slide will be a picture!

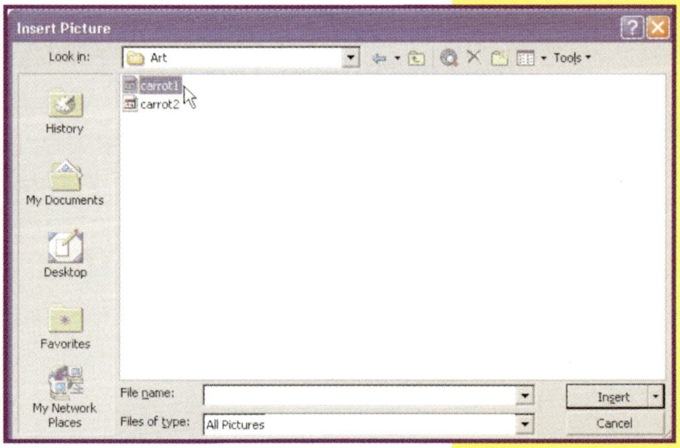

PowerPoint

1. Click on **New Slide**.
2. Choose **Picture** from the **Insert** menu. Then choose **From File**.
3. Find the file named *carrot1*.
4. Click on **Insert**, and the picture will appear on the slide.
5. Save your work.

AppleWorks

1. Click on Slide 3 in the **Controls** window.
2. Choose **Insert** from the **File** menu.
3. Under **File Format**, use the arrow to select **All Available**.
4. Find the file named *carrot1*.
5. Click on **Insert**.
6. Save your work.

Slide 3

You can change the picture's size or position. Here is what Slide 3 looks like.

Slide 4

Now that you have added a picture once, you can do it as many times as you want! On Slide 4, add the file named carrot2.

1. Create a new slide or click on Slide 4.
2. Insert the file named *carrot2*.
3. Save your work.

PART 2

Date Lines

Now we have a long empty line that is waiting to be filled with information. We need to add dates. We need to add lines that connect the dates to the timeline. Let's do it!

1. Put your cursor under the line at the left side of the page.
2. Tap **Enter**.
3. Type *1875*.
4. Tap the **Tab** key three times and type *1880*.

Now add the years 1885, 1890, 1895, and 1900. Make sure that there is equal space between these dates.

Now we need to connect the dates to the timeline.

5. Click on the **Line** tool. Put your cursor above the year 1875.
6. Draw a short vertical line from the timeline to the date.

Repeat this step for each date. Double-click on the Line tool to keep it selected. Then you will not have to click on it each time you draw a line.

7. Save your work.

Quick Check

Your timeline should look like this.

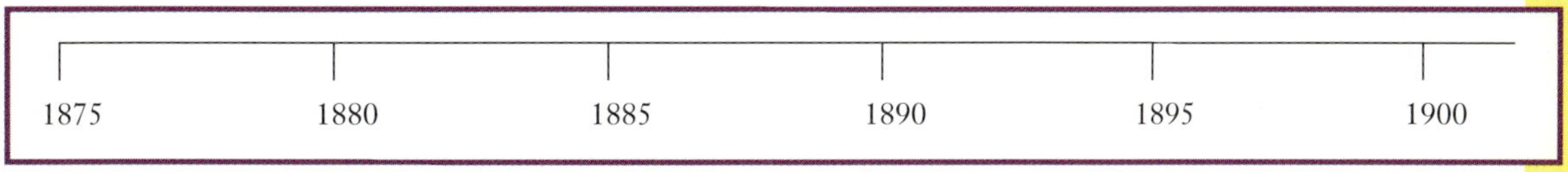

*Use your **Undo** button if you need to make corrections!*

*In Word, select the line, then hold down the **Alt** or **Option** key to move the line to a specific location.*

PART 3

A Change of Color

Now let's change the background color of our slides. I want to use green because so many plants are green.

PowerPoint

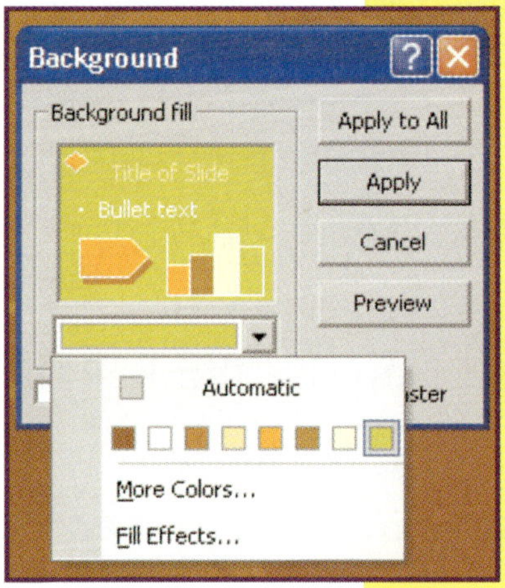

1. Choose **Background** from the **Format** menu.
2. Click on the **Background fill** drop-down list and choose green.
3. Click on **Apply to All**.
4. Save the file again.

AppleWorks

1. Click on the text box in Slide 2.
2. Choose **Edit Background** from the **Options** menu.
3. Click on the **Color palette** button on the **Tools** window.
4. Click on a green color.
5. Choose **Edit Background** from the **Options** menu to turn off background editing.
6. Save your work.

PowerPoint

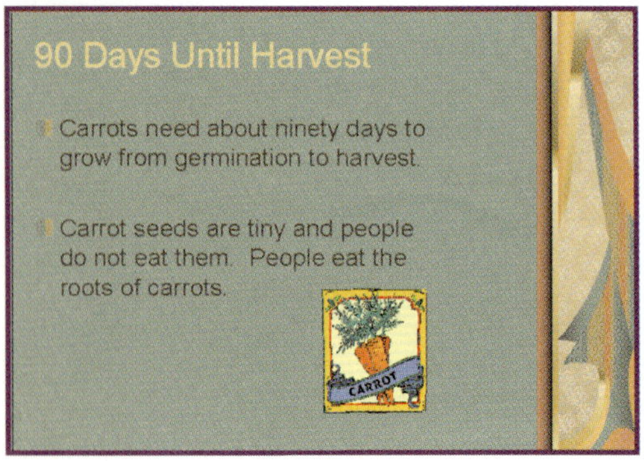

Slide 2

AppleWorks

Slide 2

PART 3

Add the Inventions

Great! Now it is time to add the inventions and the dates they were invented. Mr. Edison told me that his favorite invention was the phonograph. He invented it in 1877. Let's put this on the timeline now.

1. Click on the **Line** tool.
2. Put your cursor above the timeline between the years 1875 and 1880. Draw a short vertical line that intersects the timeline.

Good job! Now you need to add the word* phonograph *above this line.

Word

3. Click on the **Text Box** button in your toolbar. 
4. Click and drag to insert a small box above the short vertical line.
5. Click in the box and type the word ***phonograph***.
6. Save the file.

AppleWorks

3. Click on the **Text** tool in the **Tools** window. 
4. Hold down the **Alt** or **Option** key and draw a text frame above the vertical line where you want to type the text.
5. Type the word ***phonograph***.
6. Save the file.

You can move and resize a text box just as you do a graphic. Click on the text box first. Then you can move it or resize it!

Quick Check

Your timeline should look like this.

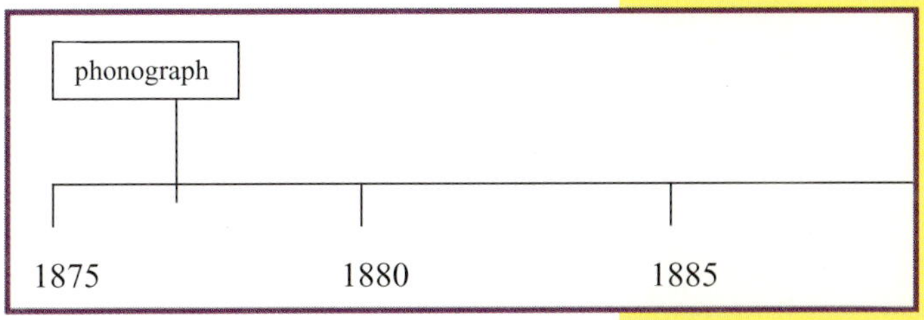

PART 2

Vegetable Facts

Now we are ready for our second slide. I want to add facts about carrots.

PowerPoint

1. To add a new slide, click on the **New Slide** button on your toolbar.
2. In the title text box, type ***90 Days Until Harvest***.
3. Click on the next text box or bullet and type ***Carrots need about ninety days to grow from germination to harvest.***
4. Click on the next text box or bullet. Type ***Carrot seeds are tiny and people do not eat them. People eat the roots of carrots.***
5. Add clip art.
6. Save your work.

AppleWorks

1. Click on Slide 2.
2. Select the text in the title box, and type ***90 Days Until Harvest***.
3. Select all the text in the text box and type ***Carrots need about ninety days to grow from germination to harvest.***
4. Tap the **Return** key. Type ***Carrot seeds are tiny and people do not eat them. People eat the roots of carrots.***

In AppleWorks, you can resize the text box. Choose ***Unlock*** *from the* ***Arrange*** *menu and then click and drag one of the box corners. Try it!*

Great job! Does your second slide look like this? We are on our way to a great slide show.

PowerPoint

AppleWorks

Excellent! Now add the following inventions to your timeline.

1879	electric light bulb
1891	motion picture camera
1896	fluorescent electric lamp

After you type each invention, you can choose a different font and font size for the words. Add some color too!

7. Save your work.

Quick Check

Does your timeline look like this? If not, make any changes now.

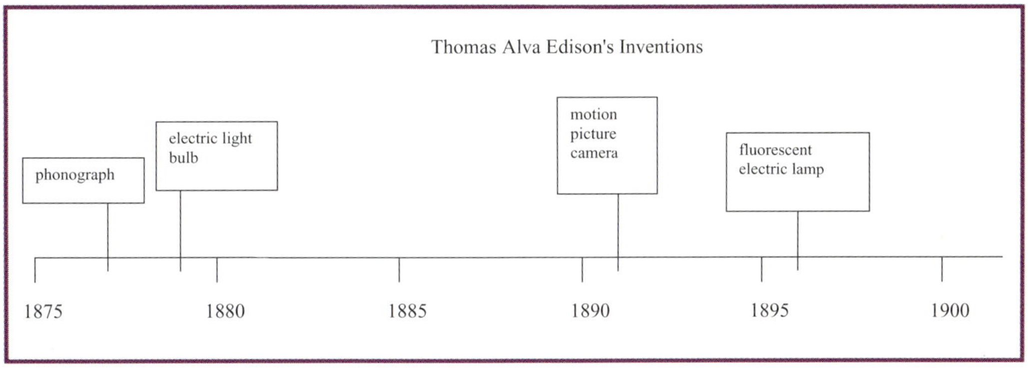

On Your Own

Edison had many bright ideas, including the invention of an electric pen in 1874 and a talking doll in 1890. Add another one of Edison's inventions to your timeline. Add graphics to your timeline. Find clip art or pictures and insert them below the dates.

AppleWorks

1. Open AppleWorks.
2. Click on the **Templates** tab.
3. Click on *All About Presentation*.

Two slides have been created, but you will need to create five new slides.

4. Click on the **Master** tab in the **Controls** window.
5. Click on Slide 1.
6. Click on the **Slide** tab.
7. Click on the **Plus** (+) button five times to create five new slides.
8. Delete the slides with a dragonfly and lizard by clicking on the slide and then clicking on the **Minus** (–) button.
9. Save your slide show as *plants11*.

Now we are ready to type the title into Slide 1.

1. Type *How Carrots Grow* in the Slide 1 title box.

If you are using AppleWorks, select the text and then begin typing. You may need to change the font size to 48 points.

2. In the next box, type *The Basics of Flowering Plants*.

If you are using AppleWorks, delete the other bullets.

3. Insert clip art of a carrot on Slide 1.
4. Save your work.

Slide 1 may look like this. We are off to a great start!

Slide 1

Bernie's Typing Activities

Key each drill line twice; key each paragraph once.

Skill Building

balanced-hand sentences

1. Glen paid the men for the work they did.
2. Nancy may sit by the dock with the maid.
3. I own the foal in the field by the lake.
4. The box with the ducks is by the mantle.
5. I may name an official to work for them.

Who Am I?

I am a little boy who lost my parents when I was a baby. I now live with my aunt and uncle. They spoil their son and do not treat me very well.

I have never had a birthday party. My room is just a tiny closet under the stairs. I am quite a famous wizard. Who am I?

Project 11

Create a Science Slide Show

In my science class, I am learning about plants and how they grow. Each student is making a slide show to teach the class about how a plant grows. My plant is the carrot!

You can help me make the slide show. Your slide show will be informative and attractive, because you will use a template, change backgrounds, and add transitions between slides. Let's get started!

PART 1

How Does Your Garden Grow?

First, you will need to pick a template. I have chosen **Kimono**. ***Your program may have different templates from mine. Just choose one you like.***

PowerPoint

1. Open PowerPoint.
2. Choose **New** from the **File** menu.
3. Click on **From Design Template** in the task pane, or click on the **Design Templates** tab.
4. Choose the *Kimono* template.
5. Save your slide show as *plants11*.

Side Trips with Blueberry and Jess

Social Studies

Create Create or draw another timeline about a different inventor. Follow the steps you used in this project. Add a title to your timeline, and write a paragraph about the life of this inventor.

Art

Draw Use the draw tools to create a certificate for a friend or family member. The certificate might be for a job well done, a sports achievement, or just to recognize a good friend. Use Landscape orientation.

Project 11

Graphics and Multimedia

Science in the Garden

In this project you will:

- Create a slide show
- Change backgrounds
- Insert graphics
- Use transitions between slides
- Set the time to advance slides
- Move a slide

Word Power

advance

background

template

transition

GLOSSARY

A

address the location to which an e-mail message is sent

Address bar the bar at the top of the Internet window where the URL appears

advance to move from one slide to the next slide in a slide show

align to make text in a paragraph line up on the left or right or to center it

AutoShape a menu in the Drawing toolbar that gives you a choice of graphics

Autosum a button on the toolbar for adding numbers in a spreadsheet

average the middle point of a group of numbers

B

Back button a button that helps you move back to a Web page that you have already seen

background the area of a computer screen that is not covered by letters or graphics

Backspace key a key on the keyboard used to erase the letter, number, space, or symbol one space to the left of the cursor

banner the headline with the name of a newspaper and the date in large, bold letters

bookmark a Web address saved by an Internet browser program

bullet a symbol used to indicate an item in a list

C

cable an electrical cord that connects parts of a computer system

callout a caption that describes a graphic or part of a graphic

Caps Lock a key on the keyboard that locks to type all uppercase letters

CD-ROM drive a device that reads information on a CD-ROM

cell an individual box within a spreadsheet, occurring where a column and a row meet

chart the presentation of data in a graphic form

cite to give credit to the source of information

clip art a collection of pictures and designs that can be added to a document

clipboard the computer's temporary memory where cut or copied data is stored

column a vertical row of boxes on a spreadsheet, usually labeled with a letter

column heading a label or words used to name a column in a spreadsheet

copy to duplicate data to put in another place in a document

Copy button a button used to copy, but not remove, text in a document in order to move it

copyright the right that allows people who create works, such as books, music, and pictures, to protect them so no one can use them without the owner's permission

CPU (Central Processing Unit) the hardware that enables computers to use data

Currency button the button in a spreadsheet program that formats numbers as dollars and cents

cursor a graphic symbol on a screen that shows where the mouse is moved

cut to remove data so it can be put in a different place

D

data information such as words, numbers, or pictures

database a software program used to organize a collection of related information on a topic

delete to erase

Delete key a key on the keyboard used to erase a letter, word, highlighted text, or graphic

digital camera a camera that stores images and can be linked to a computer to transfer photographs directly to the screen

disk drive a device that reads and writes data on a disk

document also called a file; pages, such as a letter or a report, created on a computer

E

e-mail electronic mail; messages that are sent and received by computers

emoticon a typed symbol used to show expression; see also *smiley*

ergonomics the way people work with machines so they do not harm themselves

F

field a place where one piece of information, such as a first name or a phone number, is entered in a database

file also called a document; pages, such as a letter or a report, created on a computer

Fill tool a paint tool used to add color to an object

Find/Change command a command that helps you find characters or words in a document and change them

floppy disk a thin disk that stores information

folder a place to store and organize files

font the style of letters, numbers, and symbols in a document

font size the size of letters, numbers, and symbols in a document

format to change the font style, color, size, and font

formula a math equation used in a spreadsheet

formula bar a bar at the top of a spreadsheet that shows the text in a highlighted cell

function a menu command in Excel that lists mathematical formulas

G

graph a graphic of numbers created from spreadsheet data; also called a chart

graphic a picture, drawing, or design

H

hardware parts of a computer system such as the keyboard, monitor, and computer

home page the first page of a Web site

hyperlink an underlined or colored word or words or a picture that connects or links one Web page with another

I

icon a picture that stands for a file or folder

Inbox a folder where e-mail messages are received and stored

infographic a document that includes information and graphics

insert to add letters, words, or other information in a document

Internet a large network that connects computers all over the world

Internet browser software a program that allows computer users to move from one Web page to another on the Internet

K

keyboard a set of keys used to type letters, numbers, and symbols into the computer

L

Landscape orientation an arrangement of information on a page that is wider than it is tall

layout the way that text and images are arranged on a page

Layout menu a menu command in an AppleWorks database

legend information that explains how to read a chart

line graph a graph that shows how data changes over time

Line tool a drawing tool used to draw lines on a page

List layout a menu in AppleWorks that shows a database in table format

M

margin the space between the edge of the paper and the text

menu a list of commands that tell the computer what to do

monitor a machine that shows computer information on a screen

mouse a device moved across the top of a desk that controls the cursor or pointer on the computer screen

N

navigate to go where you want to go in the computer

netiquette the rules of good behavior when using e-mail

O

offline not connected to the Internet

online connected to the Internet

operator a symbol in a spreadsheet that represents a specific action, for example + (addition), – (subtraction), and * (multiplication)

Outbox a folder where e-mail messages are stored until they are sent

Oval tool a drawing or paint tool used to draw circles and ovals on a page

P

paste to insert cut or copied text in a document

Paste button a button used to insert cut or copied text in a document

printer a machine that prints a document created on a computer

program instructions inside a computer that tell it what to do

pull-down menu also called a drop-down menu; a list of commands in a program

R

range cells in a spreadsheet that are next to each other in a column or row

record a group of fields about one topic in a database

Rectangle tool a drawing or paint tool used to draw squares or rectangles on a page

Replace command a command that allows you to replace words or characters that you have found and selected in a document

Restore Down button the button that returns a window to its original size

row a horizontal row of boxes on a spreadsheet, usually labeled with a number

row heading a label or words used to name a row in a spreadsheet

ruler a bar in a word processing program that is used to set margins and tabs

S

scanner a device that takes a picture of an image that exists outside the computer and sends the information to the computer as a file

search to have the computer look for something, either a file or data within a file

search engine a program that searches the Internet for specific keywords and returns a list of Web pages where the keywords are found

select to highlight text to change it

shading coloring used to make part of a document, table, or graph stand out

shortcut keys two or more keys pressed at the same time to command the computer to complete a task

sizing handles the points on a graphic used to make the graphic bigger or smaller

slide one page in a presentation program

slide show a group of slides put in order and displayed one after another

smiley a typed symbol used to show expression; see also *emoticon*

software a computer program that tells the computer what to do

sort to organize items in some kind of order

Sort Ascending button a button that will alphabetize a selected list of words

spelling checker a tool that finds and corrects misspelled words in a document

spreadsheet a software program that works with numbers

spreadsheet cursor a blinking, cross-shaped character that shows where the next typed letter, number, or symbol will appear on a spreadsheet

style the way typed words look, such as bold, italicized, or underlined

T

tab a spot marked on a ruler for indenting text

Tab key a key used to move from cell to cell in a spreadsheet. The Tab key will also indent text.

table a grid with information shown in rows and columns

template a file used to create documents that look alike

text box a preset box in a slide template

Text Box button a button on the Drawing toolbar used to draw boxes

text frame a frame, drawn with the text tool, that holds text

text insertion point the blinking line or I-beam shaped like a capital I on the screen where the next typed letter, number, space, or symbol will appear

Text tool a tool used to add text to pictures on a page

thesaurus an electronic reference tool used to look up synonyms

timeline a horizontal or vertical line marked with a series of dates to show when events occurred

timing the amount of time between slides in a slide show

toolbar a row of command buttons across the top of a software program; clicking a toolbar button is a shortcut for using the menu commands

transition the method that a slide show program uses to move from one slide to another

U

URL (Uniform Resource Locator) the location or address of a Web page; starts with http://

W

Web address the location of a file or Web site on the Internet

Web browser a software program that connects to the Internet

Web page a document on the Internet that can have text, graphics, sound, and video

Web site a group of related Web pages, images, and other files

word processor a software program used to create and edit documents

worksheet a spreadsheet file

wrap to place words around a graphic image in a document

WWW (World Wide Web) a part of the Internet that has Web pages with links to other Web pages

Z

Zoom box the button that changes the size of a window